Health Cent$

Health Cent$

Isn't it time your Health Insurance wrote you a check??

Jeffrey Taragano

Writers Club Press
San Jose New York Lincoln Shanghai

Health Cent$
Isn't it time your Health Insurance wrote you a check??

Writers Club Press
an imprint of iUniverse.com, Inc.

For information address:
iUniverse.com, Inc.
5220 S 16th, Ste. 200
Lincoln, NE 68512
www.iuniverse.com

ISBN: 0-595-20030-3

Printed in the United States of America

CONTENTS

ABOUT THE AUTHOR

JEFF TARAGANO:

In his role as Chief Operating Officer, Jeff Taragano has saved corporations millions of dollars.

He achieved this through corporate reorganization and cost reduction techniques—obtaining substantial refunds by auditing bills, recovering overcharges and improving systems for companies and individuals over his 20 year career.

But it wasn't until his son made over 75 visits to various doctors in one year that he realized how many mistakes doctors, medical billing companies and insurance companies make. By the end of that year, when the errors had amounted to over $3,000 in overcharges—and subsequent refunds—he realized he had developed a system other people could benefit from, too. That system turned into *Health Cent$*.

By using the methods described in this book, he saved over $15,000 in seven years for himself and his family. Using the same system, he saved even more money for his friends, relatives and co-workers.

ABOUT THE EDITOR

KAREN DALE WOLMAN:

Karen Dale Wolman's expertise as a writer includes three books, over 200 articles and many years as an investigative journalist. She has researched and written about healthcare issues for national magazines, and advocated for healthcare rights, as well as working in the healthcare field, for an organization that makes sure people get the healthcare and coverage they are entitled to.

Her books and articles have been published and distributed in four countries. She has been granted fellowships and awards for her work from the *University of Southern California, the Helene Wurlitzer Foundation of New Mexico, the Florida State Arts Council* and *Ibelle Magazine.* She holds a Master's degree in Professional Writing from USC.

She and her family have saved thousands of dollars by using the system pioneered in this book.

DISCLAIMER

This book is designed to be used as a series of guidelines for making sure you get the full financial benefits of your health insurance policy.

The information in this book is as accurate as we know it to be. Healthcare and insurance laws are constantly changing. Many offer increased consumer protection.

The authors do not guarantee the outcome of any particular situation, nor do they guarantee any particular dollar amount of savings.

They can only tell you that the trillion dollar industry makes $40 billion in errors every year. If you go to the hospital just once, a refund or bill reduction of several thousand dollars is not unheard of by using the methods in this book.

INTRODUCTION

If the healthcare industry is ripping you off, you're not alone.

Physicians, hospitals, clinics and labs routinely overcharge patients or bill both patients and their insurance companies for the same services. If you didn't know better, you'd pay the same bills your insurance company already did. But this book will show you how to spot illegitimate charges like these and not only save thousands of dollars, but get money from past overpayments refunded to you.

A recent *Money Magazine* article revealed that Americans are overcharged a whopping $10 billion every year for medical care.[1] Equifax Services, which placed the abuses at $20 billion, found that an astonishing 97% of medical bills contain errors.[2]

The real number is probably closer to $40 billion, or over $500 per insured family, per year. With only a 3% chance that your bill is actually correct, you need a book like this to make sure you don't overpay, and get your money back if you already did.

Errors and overcharges are the norm, not the exception. The frenzied pace of medical billing results in mistakes that contribute to $40 billion a year in errors in a trillion dollar industry. But the healthcare industry gets away with this because the average person isn't an expert in understanding complicated medical codes, billing procedures or recovering overpayments because of other people's mistakes.

---

1. Money Magazine.
2. Equifax Services.

The increase of health clinics and urgent care centers that see patients on demand but charge full price up front have worsened the problem. More and more people utilize this type of care because they are tired of the long waits for appointments at their primary physician's office, but after the medical care, they have to then figure out what they were really supposed to pay and try to get the money back from the medical center or their insurer.

Most people are afraid of challenging insurance companies, doctors, hospitals, labs and medical administrators, so they just pay the bills, even when they don't understand them.

But you don't have to do that anymore. With this book, you'll learn:
- how to identify requests for double payments so you don't pay bills your insurance company already did;
- how to understand exactly what you're covered for;
- how to decipher complicated medical bills so you can figure out what you really owe;
- how to get excessive charges removed from your accounts;
- what questions to ask when you don't understand;
- how to keep track of your deductibles or co-payments;
- how to use cafeteria plans, saving you up to an additional 40%, or more, depending on your tax rate.
- *even how to get refunds for incorrect bills you paid years ago.*

Once you know how you're being overcharged, you can stop paying inflated bills, get refunds for past mistakes and no longer be a victim of excessive medical bills.

Many people routinely pay incorrect bills or accept coverage denials because they don't know they have any other choice. This book shows that you do. By using the simple guidelines and tips in the following chapters, you'll learn not only how to identify incorrect charges and get them removed from your records, but how to receive refunds for past payments you didn't really have to make, and much, much more.

By providing you with the information you need in a simple, easy-to-understand format, getting refunds will be easier than getting a doctor's appointment. You can, for instance, clearly see a detailed overview of what coverage you're entitled to on the benefit summary given to every consumer by every insurance agency. The benefit summary lays out, in two pages, what your coverage is, what you have to pay and what you don't. If you can't find yours, it's easily available with a phone call to your insurer or Human Resources Department.

No matter what type of insurance policy you have, *Health Cent$* will explain the most common ways you get overcharged. A simple written referral from your doctor that doesn't make it into the insurance company's files means a bill you shouldn't get. An unitemized bill from a hospital may charge you for medical care—like the surgeon and the anesthesiologist—which you already paid for.

This practical workbook is designed to tackle these problems by clarifying your coverage, identifying billing errors and tracking the billing and payment process.

Getting refunds is easy, once you know what to look for.

In some of the more common abuses in the medical billing industry, patients are billed twice for the same service—once from the hospital and again by the doctor; are denied coverage because procedures are miscoded; have their claims turned down because someone didn't do the proper paperwork.

Did you know that you could also get discounts on your medical charges? You are entitled to these discounts through your insurance company, but you probably won't get them unless you ask. While chapter 7 explains this in further detail, you are entitled to reduced fees called *reasonable and customary charges* for your medical bills. Doctors, labs, clinics and hospitals have high rates they charge the general public. But they all contract with insurance companies at lower rates. You will usually get charged the higher rate, unless you complain. We'll show you how to do that.

A call to your insurance company or simply reading your insurance statement will reveal what the reasonable and customary rate is, and a second call to your doctor's office, the lab, the hospital or the clinic will get the charge reduced. Now you know that the policy exists, and you now know you can get your bill reduced. You should not need this book to find that out, but unfortunately you do.

The same types of errors and overcharges occur no matter which part of the country you live in. This book will show you exactly what to look for and how to avoid paying for other people's mistakes.

Our system, *Health Cent$*, will save you money by teaching you to easily identify errors and overcharges in doctor, hospital, clinic, lab and insurance statements.

Here's just one small example of how this book will save you money. If your doctor's office refers you for lab work—anything from a blood test to a biopsy—the lab's billing service will invoice both you and your insurance company at the same time. If you didn't know your insurance company was already paying the bill, you'd probably send a check to the lab. Now that you've read this book, you won't let that happen again. Chapter 8 will even show you how to get money back if you paid bills like this in the past.

Whether you're enrolled in an HMO, a PPO ,a split POS plan or paid for a procedure on your own, this book will help you understand your coverage and avoid paying money you don't really owe. It doesn't matter if you have an individual, employee, government, professional association, retirement, Medicaid, Medicare or COBRA plan. The easy-to-understand worksheets and form letters will make sure you don't pay a dime more than you're supposed to. Just follow the simple steps in the appropriate chapters to get reimbursed for overcharges and errors.

Each chapter goes over specific types of billing problems and errors, along with step-by-step instructions on how to either receive refunds or get charges removed from your bill.

Doing this on your own could be so complex that you probably wouldn't even bother to try, but *Health Cent$* makes it a snap. It's a simple system that will help you to understand your medical bills and show you how and when to challenge the charges.

We'll give you the simple steps you can take to save yourself a lot of money. If you want to, you can start immediately to obtain refunds, simply skip to chapter 26 and start filling in your refund worksheet.

Armed with the information in this book, often a single, ten-minute phone call or a faxed letter will make an unwarranted charge disappear from your bill. Not bad for a book that costs only $19.95.

TIPS FOR SAVING MONEY

TIPS FOR SAVING MONEY:	FOR MORE INFO, SEE:
Did you know:	
REFUNDS:	*Chapter 8*

- you can get refunds for money you paid for overcharges, duplicate billings and improper billings one, three, even five years ago?

REASONABLE AND CUSTOMARY:	*Chapter 7*

- you are entitled to a discounted rate on your medical costs? Insurance companies contract with doctors, hospitals and labs for lower prices. These reasonable and customary rates, not the higher amount that usually appears on your bill, are all you have to pay.

PROCEDURE CODES:	*Chapter 3*

- if you catch a simple miscoding of a procedure on an invoice it can mean hundreds or thousands of dollars in your pocket?

**ITEMIZED
BILLING:** *Chapter 5*

- you can challenge that unitemized bill you got when you left the hospital and get charges removed from your account? Since most unitemized bills contain errors, double-billing you for services you were already billed for separately or charging you for tests or treatment you never received, combing through the specific charges can save you thousands of dollars.

**THE
EMERGENCY
ROOM:** *Chapter 12*

- if you went to the emergency room, then got admitted to the hospital, your emergency room bill will probably be waived?

- if you go for follow-up care at the emergency room instead of your doctor's office, your insurance can deny payment, even if the ER doctor told you to come back in a couple of days? Call your regular doctor and either make an appointment, or get a referral to a specialist, and you will get that care paid for.

TRAVEL: *Chapter 15*

      - if you got sick when you were traveling—for business or for pleasure—you can get the medical bills covered, even if you went outside of your network?

**CLAIM
DENIALS:**   *Chapter 11*

      - just because your insurance company has denied your claim doesn't mean you have to pay the bill? You have rights.

REFERRALS: *Chapter 13*

      - if your doctor provides a written referral to a specialist, you can get that visit covered, too?

LAB BILLS: *Chapter 5*

      - if you have an HMO, you probably don't have to pay the bill sent to you by the lab?

**HMO
NIGHTMARES:**   *Chapter 21*

      - when your doctor leaves the plan, you still have rights? You may be entitled to see that same doctor for your illness or injury, without paying extra, even if it is "out of network."

BILLING ERRORS: *Chapter 3*

 - most billing errors can be removed from your account with a simple ten minute phone call?

ANNUAL LIMITS: *Chapter 19*

 - you may not have to pay medical bills all year long because there is an annual dollar limit to your out-of-pocket costs?

FIGHTING BACK: *Chapters 11 and 24*

 - you can get a charge removed from your bill, even after your insurance company has denied the request for payment?

GET ORGANIZED:
 - if you pay the right amount when you leave the doctor's office, you won't get a bill, so there won't be any place for mistakes?

Health Cent$

CHECK IT OUT:

> - you should make sure your doctor's office has your most up-to-date insurance information? If your insurance coverage is listed incorrectly, you may be losing benefits.

CHAPTER 1—READ THE BILL:
THERE IS ONLY A 3% CHANCE IT IS CORRECT

The first thing you need to do is read every bill you get from every lab, every doctor's office, every clinic and every hospital.

The lab may bill you for tests that were ordered but never done; the doctor's office may have charged you for a vaccination that should have been included in the office visit charge; the clinic may have used the wrong code; and the hospital bill probably contains more errors than correct charges. All of this results in billing errors.

Remember the numbers:
- Only 3% of bills are correct;
- 97% of bills contain errors;

So there's a 97% chance that someone owes you money.

The following chapters detail the specific problems, how to locate them and how to get them corrected, but here's a brief summary of the most common errors and how to spot them.

If the hospital bill says, "For Services Rendered," "Emergency Room Visit," "Lab Tests," or something equally vague with just a total and no details, you don't know what they're asking you to pay for. You can't find incorrect charges if the specific charges aren't listed. What you can do is call and ask for an itemized bill.

That should get sent to you within a couple of weeks. Incredible, isn't it, that a simple request for an itemized invoice—a single piece of paper they can produce at the touch of a button—may take three or four weeks? But they don't want to make it easy for you. They want you to give up and pay the padded bill. But you won't.

Once you have the itemized bill, read through the list of charges. You'll not only find duplicate charges; you'll probably find charges for services you never received. An entire chapter, number 5, is dedicated to helping you identify and eliminate duplicate charges. Chapter 6 will tell you about finding and eliminating phantom charges on your hospital bill.

Your healthcare bill may also be charging you for services that were never provided, even by your regular and trusted doctor. Take a look at the following example.

A breast cancer patient who received regular chemotherapy treatments also received bills from her primary care doctor, billing her for "supervising treatments" for each chemotherapy session. The problem? Her regular doctor was on the other side of town and had nothing to do with the chemotherapy.

A discussion with your doctor, and/or a letter, can get charges like this removed from your bill.

This book will also show you how to find benefits you didn't even know you had. Your insurance policy, for example, may charge a co-payment of $100 for only the first five days of hospital care. If you were hospitalized for twelve days, you owe $500, not $1200, an error that would cost you $700 if you didn't know to look for it. If you were admitted through the emergency room, make sure you weren't billed for both emergency and inpatient care. Some insurance companies waive the emergency room fee if you are admitted to the hospital, but most people don't know that.

It's tough to keep a log of tests, medications and physician visits when you're sick or in pain, but the more you know about your hospital visit, the less you'll have to pay. The norm is for hospital bills to contain charges for services you never got.

Were you billed for five days of IV when you were only hooked up for three? Did your doctor cancel lab tests, but the hospital billed you anyway?

Once you identify charges like these, you can have them removed from your bill.

Ask the friends and relatives who visited you to help fill in whatever you don't remember. This can help you recall that the canceled lab test you were billed for was on Tuesday afternoon, when Aunt Sally visited, and the doctor didn't examine you until the afternoon of your second day, when your best friend sent flowers. Tests, exams and treatments are all listed on your chart, so anything that's not in there didn't happen.

Hospitals hate to pull charts, but they'll do it if you insist. And if you insist, you'll probably find that several things you were billed for didn't happen. It's an easy way to get hundreds or thousands of dollars removed from your bill.

After you identify all double billing and charges for services you didn't receive, look for anything you don't recognize, then call and ask for an explanation. After all, if you don't understand it, you can't question it. Ask to have all terms defined and explained to you. It's tough asking questions like this, but it's your right to find out if you were billed for a specialist who never reviewed your case, five daily doctor visits when the doctor showed up only twice, lab tests you didn't have, or charges that belong to other patients. Only after you understand the charges will you be able to get the incorrect ones removed.

Once you identify which charges are wrong, ask the hospital to remove them. One or two 10 minute phone calls could be worth hundreds or thousands of dollars to you. If they want your request in writing, the form letters in chapter 25 will help you correspond with the hospital.

Use the same procedure for the bill you received for the emergency room. Particularly in that rushed environment, mistakes are frequent.

Do the same thing for every bill you get from every doctor's office, every clinic, and every lab. Then go back and look over your bills for the past one, two, three, even five years. If the bills you paid were incorrect, you can get your money refunded. Chapter 8 will show you how.

CHAPTER 2—COMMON BILLING ERRORS YOU WON'T BELIEVE

Medical billing services, doctors' offices, hospitals, labs, clinics and insurance companies make mistakes all the time—to the tune of at least several billion dollars a year, according to respected NBC news anchor Mike Jensen.

"You shouldn't have to hire a team of outside interpreters to go through your health bills," Jensen explains, "but obviously you do. Red tape and overcharging is grinding down Americans for billions of dollars a year in medical bills they should never have to pay."

But you can't catch these errors unless you know what to look for. Equifax Services discovered, "After auditing forty thousand hospital bills, more than 97% contained errors. Mistakes on bills can be spotted only if you receive an itemized bill, and nine times out of ten a hospital will not give you an itemized bill unless you ask for it." We've devoted an entire chapter (chapter 5) to make sure you don't get ripped off this way.

With only a 3% chance your bill is correct, you have to go over each medical bill with a fine-toothed comb. With the same types of errors happening over and over again, they're easy to find, once you know what to look for.

Sometimes your account isn't credited properly; sometimes it isn't credited at all. It could be the fault of a medical billing service, a doctor's office, a hospital, a clinic, a lab or an insurance company. But the end result is the same: you get billed for a service you never got or already paid for because of someone else's carelessness or mistake. That's money you don't owe.

There are about a dozen types of common errors you should look out for. Here are the kind of mistakes that happen all the time:

The doctor, hospital, lab and/or billing service:

- tries to charge you for tests that the lab already billed your insurance company for;
- submits the wrong procedure or diagnosis code, resulting in your insurance company rejecting your claim completely or underpaying for your medical costs. It's not unusual for them to code your $1200 MRI as a $60 x-ray. If you don't catch the error, you're out over a thousand dollars!
- charges you an amount much higher than the reasonable and customary fee allowed by the insurance company. For chronic problems like allergies, which require weekly shots, this can mean you get overcharged hundreds of dollars in just a few months;
- does not credit your account with the payment received from your insurance company; you get billed for it instead;
- charges you for a procedure you never even had;
- almost never sends you correct statements because they are too backlogged; it's just about impossible to reconcile your payments with their statements without a book like this;
- does not submit the bill to the correct insurance company or with the correct group or plan number.
- does not calculate or post entries to your account properly, resulting in a mathematical error, or does not submit the bill on your behalf to your insurance company;
- never sends you an itemized bill, so you don't know how much you really owe;
- incorrectly charges you for someone else's bill;
- does not record a payment you've made, so you keep getting bills.

Errors can also happen on the other end. Here's what to look for:
Your insurance company:
- charges you for services that were never even performed;
- does not receive a bill from your doctor, doctor's billing service or the lab, so they never pay it, but you get billed by your doctor. Either you pay a bill for money you don't owe, or you get hounded by a collection agency;
- pays on an incorrect code, so you get a lot less money than you deserve;
- doesn't pay a bill because it gets lost on someone's desk or applied to another patient's account;
- never received the paperwork for a referral to a specialist, so it doesn't bother to pay the bill;
- does not apply the correct co-payment;
- does not credit your deductible properly;
- inputs the wrong data from the bill, so your claim either gets underpaid or rejected completely;
- tells you that a doctor isn't in the network when he or she really is; you get billed for hundreds of dollars for an out-of-network visit instead of charged a minor co-payment;
- does not have your primary care physician in the system yet; it can take the insurance company four to six months just to process your physician into their system, while you've been going to the doctor the whole time;
- pays the doctor directly after you already paid the doctor, so now the doctor owes you money; if you don't complain, you won't get the refund;
- doesn't tell you when you've reached your annual maximum out-of-pocket limit and you don't owe anything else for the rest of the year;

- turns down your claim for a diagnostic test that's not regularly covered at your age, even though your doctor ordered it because of specific risk factors;
- tells you the length of your hospital stay is not covered when federal law demands that your insurer pay for it!

CHAPTER 3—CHALLENGING BILLS, CHALLENGING DECISIONS

Just because your insurance company turned down your provider's request for payment, doesn't mean you have to pay the bill.

Just because your provider's office sends you a statement of charges, doesn't mean you really owe the money. It may not even be correct. In fact, odds are it's wrong.

Every bill, every decision in the healthcare industry can be challenged. You just need to know where the errors are, so you can get them removed from your account.

Once you know why they don't want to pay, you'll know how to fight. Is it a simple mistake, missing paperwork, or do you need to challenge your insurance company's decision?

A simple typographical error on a procedure code could mean a difference of hundreds of dollars. So when your insurance company turns you down, they may be turning you down for the wrong thing. Or maybe they think the procedure you had was unnecessary, or they don't have the written documentation for prior approval.

First, call your insurance company and ask for an explanation. If there are codes on your bill, ask what they mean. If they answer you in technical-speak, ask what it means in plain English. If their answer isn't clear enough, get your doctor's office to explain it to you.

If the wrong procedure code was entered in the computer, you can get it corrected very easily. Ask what the code means and you'll know if the decision was based on the procedure you actually had (injection, x-ray, etc.) or something else. Say your vaccination was coded as an allergy shot. If allergy shots aren't covered under your policy but vaccinations are, when the procedure code is corrected, your bill will be cleared. If your ultrasound was coded as an MRI, a much more expensive test, you may get a bill for thousands of dollars. One phone call, or a simple letter, will fix it.

Some treatments require clearance in advance. Unless it was an emergency, you probably need advance, written approval for a referral to a specialist, many diagnostic tests or treatments like physical therapy. Depending on your insurer, the approval can be granted by your primary care physician or it may have to go through a review committee. If any of the paperwork work gets lost, or wasn't done properly in the first place, the claim will be denied. Get a copy of the referral from your doctor, send it to your insurer, and you'll get your bills covered.

Other times, the insurance company may challenge the validity of the procedure you had. If that's the case, have your doctor write a letter explaining why the test or the treatment was necessary. Insurance companies have a formal appeals process, if you need to go that far. Chapter 24 will instruct you on what to do in that case. But often, a letter from your doctor will get them to cover the costs.

Be just as careful with any money you're asked to pay directly at your doctor's office. If your co-payment covers the entire office visit, you don't have to pay extra for x-rays or shots. For regular treatments like allergy shots, this can save you hundreds of dollars a year.

Your summary of benefits, which is a simple two page overview, will lay this out for you clearly. Bring a copy when you go for your appointments and the problem should get solved right there. If you overpaid in the past, fax or mail a copy to your doctor and you'll get a refund. They can't fight with written policy.

Also be sure that you really received everything you're charged for when you were in the hospital or at a clinic. If a lab slip or prescription order for another patient ends up in your chart, you'll receive a bill. If your doctor decided you didn't need all the tests or all the treatments you were originally scheduled for, you may get billed anyway. When this happens to you, start with a phone call. If that's not enough, send a letter. It'll get you a check in the mail.

The following chapters detail how to challenge all types of errors and decisions in the healthcare industry. Is your hospital bill wrong? Read chapter 6. Have the lab and the insurance company billed you for the same test? Chapter 5 will tell you how to solve that. Problems with your dental coverage? Chapter 23 will tell you what to do.

CHAPTER 4—HOW DOES THE BILLING SYSTEM WORK TO RIP YOU OFF?

How many times have you been in the supermarket and found yourself overcharged at the cash register because the price in the computer is higher than the price on the shelf? Pointing out the error to the cashier gets it corrected quickly.

Medical billing is no different. The mistakes are bigger and more frequent, often hundreds or thousands of dollars instead of a handful of change, but they're just as easy to catch and just as easy to get corrected. As long as you understand how the medical billing process works.

Medical billing isn't necessarily done by the doctor's office. It's usually contracted out piecemeal to medical billing services that receive a set figure per bill. These companies get paid per piece, **but they don't get any incentives for accuracy or any penalties for mistakes.** They may receive up to $6 for each bill they process, so their only incentive is to work as fast as possible.

These impersonal service companies process tens of thousands of bills a day. The goal is to input as fast as possible, and that's not good for accuracy. While you would get fired if a high percentage of your work were wrong, they just rack up the bucks.

But that's not all. Add the errors made by the insurance companies, providers hospitalities, and the number of mistakes are alarming.

The whole medical billing system is designed to fail. The amount on your bill seems to be picked out of the air, you may not understand the code, and the person who input the charges never even set foot in your doctor's office.

"If we sat down to invent a billing system to frustrate the public, we could not have done a better job," says Rick Waite of the American Hospital Association.

The bill for your provider's visit is not only most probably wrong, you can't even reach the person who sent it to you. But the problem doesn't stop there. While there are dozens of different ways a provider's invoice could reflect a billing service error, the insurance company can make the same amount of errors to compound this. No wonder the mistake rate is at 97%.

As if an error on a bill from a simple doctor's visit isn't bad enough, imagine getting a huge bill, with no explanation, after surviving the trauma of a hospitalization. If they don't list the charges, you can't challenge them, right? And you have no way of knowing if the hospital was already paid by the insurance company? Right? Wrong!

As chapters 5 and 6 detail, you can get an itemized hospital bill, go over the list of charges, identify services you didn't receive, get duplicate charges removed, and check what your insurance company already paid.

While many billing mistakes may be due to accidents and carelessness, the system itself is flawed. That's how it's designed. But don't expect them to fix it, even when they're told about the problems. After all, providers can make millions of dollars in excess charges.

Chapter 6 reveals a billing scandal to the tune of $4.2 million at a university clinic in Florida. Due to sloppy bookkeeping and a faulty computer program, which they knew about for years, the mental health clinic sent the state millions of dollars in excess bills. It took legal action on the part of the state to get the overcharges to stop.

If it can happen to the state, it can happen to you. From a private doctor to a public clinic, the system is designed to overcharge you. Once you know that, you have all the power. Instead of paying, you challenge, and you win.

One of the most common billing errors is to bill for more services than were actually provided. You can identify this easily by listing all medical appointments in a date book and keeping your receipts in one place. This will make it easy to catch a bill that charges you for six hours of therapy when you only had two, or four x-rays when you really had three.

Be particularly vigilant about cancelled appointments. The billing system may automatically charge you for an appointment, even when you didn't use it. If this happens to you, call the doctor or clinic, give them the dates, tell them the first appointment had been rescheduled, and get the charge removed from your account.

You also don't have to pay for other people's errors. If your x-ray had to be redone because it came out blurry, that's not your problem. One phone call can get a charge like that taken off your bill, or refunded if you already paid it.

Just because the system is faulty doesn't mean more money comes out of your pocket. It's all about asking and checking. Instead of assuming the charges are correct, paying them and grumbling to your friends and family—or having the bills go to collection when they aren't even accurate—this book shows you how to question, challenge and get your money back.

While the medical billing system is designed to give you as little information and take as much of your money as possible, your new system is to never assume a bill or decision is correct. You'll learn how to read every bill, ask questions for everything that isn't clear, and demand coverage or a refund when it's owed to you.

Check and challenge every single bill. That's why you bought this book: to show you how.

Look over each bill, ask for explanations, and demand that incorrect charges be removed. Not only will your bills be lower, but you can receive refunds for mistakes that happened years ago.

CHAPTER 5—DUPLICATE BILLING: DON'T PAY FOR IT TWICE

Double-billing is one of the most common "mistakes" in the medical billing industry.

Doctor's offices and hospitals routinely send bills to both patients and insurance companies. Clinics and laboratories do the same. Since most medical bills are unitemized, you won't catch the duplications unless you know what to look for. But you don't have to pay twice. Not anymore.

With a couple of phone calls, you can easily get hundreds, thousands, even tens of thousands of dollars in duplicate charges removed from your bills. After all, if your credit card tried to bill you twice for the same purchase, you'd call up and get the second charge removed right away. Why not do the same with your medical bills?

Here's how it works. Say you get lab tests or an x-ray. The same bill will get sent to both you and your insurance company. If you both pay, the lab gets paid twice, and you get cheated out of your money.

A patient in Arizona received lab bills for over $100 after a routine physical exam. Under her HMO insurance plan, one $10 co-payment covered the entire office visit, including the two lab tests. The insurance company was responsible for the lab bills, based on contracted rates. When she called the lab to complain, they said that billing her was a simple mistake and they removed the charges.

But when she called the doctor's office to tell them about the double-billing, they told her they got about 20 similar complaints a day, which is over 5,000 complaints a year. You can imagine the extent of the problem, but nobody tried to stop it. Why should they? The 5,000 people who complained every year got the duplicate bills canceled, but a much higher number paid the lab bills. Multiply that by the hundreds of doctor's office they get work from, and you can see the extent of their extra profit.

The system is set up to automatically bill everyone possible. But don't let a flawed system cost you money. Double-billing is their scam, not your responsibility.

That's why you need to double-check your coverage. Read your summary of benefits. If the medical care you received is covered, you're not responsible for paying for it. When you get billed for it anyway, call your insurance company: chances are they already received a bill—and they may have already paid it.

Armed with this information, call the lab and let them know that under your policy, its the insurer's responsibility, and the bill has either already been paid or a check will be issued soon. As the lab doesn't want too much attention focused on its double-billing practices, they won't be asking you for money anymore.

The same kind of double-billing happens with hospitals, doctor's offices and clinics. They just want to get paid and they don't care who writes the check, so they send out bills to both patient and insurer. If they get paid twice, it's a bonus for them, and you'll never know about it.

Which doesn't mean you have to write off money that you paid to double billing several years ago. Look through old bills and old policies, and you'll find money that's owed to you.

Once you uncover the double-payments, call whoever got paid twice, insist they pull old records even if they resist, and tell them you want a refund. Just fill in the blanks in the form letter in chapter 25, and you'll soon have a check in the mail.

Hospitals are the biggest culprits in the double-billing scandal. They habitually send out unitemized bills, just listing a huge lump sum, with no explanation of the charges. Most people either pay, no questions asked, or ignore the bills until they go to collection. But you don't have to do that. You don't have to pay money you don't owe, and you don't have to let your credit be ruined because you didn't pay the hospital when you already mailed the doctor a check.

What you can do is call the hospital and ask for an itemized bill. That will usually get sent to you within a couple of weeks. Once you have the bill, read through the list of charges to identify duplicate charges and charges for services you never received.

Here's what you need to do. Once you get an itemized bill, identify anything you either already paid for or received a separate bill for. For example, does the hospital bill include physician visits, a surgeon fee or the anesthesiologist when you already received a bill for those services directly from the doctor? You don't need to pay twice.

Mark off all charges on the itemized bill that you were already billed for by the doctor, the physical therapist, and the surgeon. Call the doctor and the hospital about it. Sometimes the charges will be removed over the phone, other times you may have to mail or fax a copy of the duplicate bill along with a letter.

Once you receive the bill, highlight any test or treatment you don't remember receiving. In particular, look for lab tests that were scheduled then canceled, drugs or IVs that were discontinued or stopped early, physical therapy you never got. Also look for dates and treatment that don't make sense. Where you billed for an MRI the day you were released, antibiotics before your infection was diagnosed, pain medication before you even had surgery?

But if you don't know to ask for an itemized bill, you won't get one, and you won't discover the fee for the x-ray you never got or duplicate charges for the internist or surgeon whose bill was already paid.

Chapter 6 gives even more details on whittling down hospital bills to what you really owe.

Even if you paid the same bills your insurer did several years ago, you can get your money back from the doctor or the hospital. Remember, they owe you the money. Chapter 8 will give you complete details on how to do this.

CHAPTER 6—DO HOSPITAL BILLING ERRORS MAKE YOU SICK?

Hospital billing departments are famous for sending out absurdly excessive bills. But most people are so grateful to be well, they pay the bill without questioning any of the charges. Other people ignore the bill, then start getting harassed by collection agencies for money they don't even owe.

Hospital billing practices are so atrocious, there is an entire industry devoted to obtaining refunds. They deserve a book of their own, but we will break it down for you in this chapter. Once you get the ball rolling, the rest comes easily.

It doesn't matter if you were in a public or private hospital, whether you have insurance or not, the bill probably has errors. According to Equifax Services, over 97% of all hospital bills contain errors. This means there's only a 3% chance your bill is correct.

With statistics like this, you need to question everything. You can and should get the bill reduced to the real and legitimate charges.

As chapter 5 explains, since you'll probably receive a lump sum bill with no details, no specifics to support the charges, the first step is to call and request an itemized bill.

Hospitals send out vague lump sum bills, which list a total charge but none of the services because they know most people will just pay without asking any questions. But those bills often include charges you already paid for, like physician services and surgery, which billed you separately, or they charge for services you never received. The itemized bill you get only after you request it most probably shows several charges that have already been paid by either you or your insurance company. If you or your insurer paid the surgeon directly, you don't have to pay the fee again in a lump sum hospital bill. A corrected bill is money in your pocket. This chapter, together with chapter 5, will take you through the whole process.

Another common type of overcharge is billing for more services than were actually performed. Departments like emergency medicine, intensive care and surgery are usually billed by the minute. At several hundred dollars a minute, you want to make sure the bill is accurate.

Errors frequently occur between the service department (ER, radiology, etc.) and the billing department. Other times, the computer program is faulty. Or so they say. You won't be the first one to identify the problem, but hospitals don't fix their software programs without a lawsuit. The overcharges net hospitals billions of dollars every year, so they don't have any incentive to correct the system.

BUNDLING:

Hospitals often bundle charges. This means they automatically bill for a set of services that are the norm for a particular medical event. Bundling for childbirth, for example, may automatically include IVs, anesthesia and use of the delivery room. The problem, of course, is that you may not have used all of those services. If you had natural childbirth in the birthing center, none of the above services were provided. But you need to call and insist the charges be removed from your bill.

It's not always easy, but if the billing department doesn't want to remove the charges, insist they compare the bill with your chart. If the chart doesn't say you received anesthesia, you didn't receive anesthesia, and you, or your insurer, shouldn't have to pay for it.

You may have to complain to a supervisor to get your chart pulled, but when you realize that request could save you thousands of dollars, you shouldn't have any trouble asking for the clerk's boss.

Use the same method for emergency room care. Have your bills compared with your hospital chart or the records in the actual departments that provided your medical care. You'll be appalled at the number of mistakes you find.

Hospital billing systems may be more complex than the ones in your doctor's office, but it is the same basic system. Isn't worth a few phone calls and letters to save several thousand dollars?

For the amount of money you'll save—or even get refunded to you—it's not a lot of work at all.

HOSPITAL BILLING SCANDALS THAT COST YOU MONEY:

While you're now aware of the normal types of billing errors to expect and how to deal with them, you also need to be on the lookout for the more outrageous mistakes.

No matter what kind of hospital you went to, you need to look closely at the bill. And treat outpatient clinics the same as the hospital itself. They're part of the same billing system, so the potential for mistakes and overcharges are the same.

Don't think that public hospitals are any better than for-profits, and don't expect the places with the best medical care to have the most accurate billing systems. University of California-Davis Medical Center, a large, renowned public hospital near the state capitol of Sacramento, was recently under fire for exorbitant charges billed to the parents of a young man who died after five hours of medical treatment following a deadly car accident.

His family was billed **$136 per minute** for operating room expenses and **$469 per minute** for emergency room care. At rates like these, you want to make sure you're not billed for a moment more than you were actually treated. A mistake of 22 minutes spent in the ER will cost you an extra $10,000.

The same hospital billed for Tylenol tablets at $19.50 each. Not only was the hospital's cost for the medication only $2 per tablet, the family's investigation uncovered that their son was never even given the Tylenol.

The charges that UC-Davis bills patients and their families—$19.50 for a 2 Tylenol, $65 for a $2 bottle of Betadine, $100 for a $6 drape sheet—are standard in the medical industry. You can't contest the 1,000% markup, but you can make sure you actually received everything you are being billed for.

On the other end of the country, a recent front-page headline in a Florida newspaper revealed a $4.2 million billing scandal by a university clinic: Nova Southeastern University's Community Mental Health Services, which contracted with the state.[3]

In one case, a bill was sent for 12 hours; the medical records showed the actual service was only one hour. In another case, three separate government agencies were billed for the same service. You can prevent this from happening to you by examining every bill, carefully.

The university blamed the errors and overcharges on a faulty computer program and sloppy bookkeeping. But they knew of the faulty system for years before a subpoena forced them to turn over records, fix the problems and stop overcharging.

You don't have to get a subpoena to find out exactly what care you received. A couple of phone calls should get you the information. Once you have that, you can compare the services performed with the services you were billed for. The actual bill you have to pay will be substantially reduced.

Treat scandalous hospital bills the same way you treat any incorrect bill. Read the bill, identify any questionable charges, and have them investigated.

---

3. Sun Sentinel, February 19, 1999.

First, challenge anything you know you didn't receive: the specialist who never showed up, four more hours of emergency room care than you really got, crutches you turned down because you already had a pair at home.

To avoid excessive charges for drugs or supplies you never received, have the chart pulled and verify everything. You can save anywhere from a couple of hundred to tens of thousands of dollars.

Don't let yourself be intimidated because the bill looks so official or you're so grateful for the care. You or your insurance company will pay for all legitimate charges. You just want to make sure you aren't getting ripped off.

TEACHING HOSPITALS:

You might think that a university hospital would cost less than a private hospital, but think again. Teaching hospitals—and university hospitals are teaching hospitals—perform more tests than even the most expensive of private hospitals, which means a higher bill for you. Some of them are so outrageous that insurance plans won't even cover those institutions. The system may be great for medical residents who need to learn new procedures, but it's lousy for you as the one who has to pay the bill.

Advance planning is the key. You can't do anything about the bill once you receive it, as long as it's correct, but you can be aware of the system.

Check things out when you're healthy. Call your local hospitals and ask if they are teaching hospitals. If they are, you'll probably be given more tests, along with a higher bill, when you go there. Knowing that, you may choose a different hospital for your emergency care or elective surgery.

If you live in a decent sized city, you usually have choices. While your first concern will be the quality of your medical care, price will be right there behind it.

Ask your doctor which hospitals he or she is affiliated with. Most have privileges at two or three. That gives you something to choose from.

CHAPTER 7—REASONABLE AND CUSTOMARY: ARE YOU BEING OVERCHARGED?

How often have you received a bill and not known if the amount is correct?

After all, if the bill says your exam or your test costs $125, how are you supposed to know it's not really $75?

By looking at your summary of benefits, that's how; or if the procedure isn't listed there, by calling your insurance company.

When doctors, labs, hospitals, etc. agree to work with insurance plans, they also agree to charge specific dollar amounts for specific services. These lower amounts are called *Reasonable and Customary Charges*. They are what medical care providers have contractually agreed to charge patients and insurance companies for anything from a ten minute exam to an extensive round of diagnostic tests.

Think of medical costs the same way you think of airline tickets. While the list price for a cross-country plane ticket may be $1200, no one actually pays that much. A supersaver fare of maybe $300 is all that it usually costs for the ticket. While the rate chart in a doctor's office may say $475, the real charge could be only $250.

If you wonder why your doctor would work at discounted rates, think of the numbers. It's a way for medical providers to get guaranteed business. Instead of seeing an occasional patient for $95 or filling the odd prescription for $40, a doctor, pharmacy or physical therapist will agree to accept lower rates in exchange for the huge volume of business.

But just because they've agreed, doesn't mean there won't be a "billing error." Billing services routinely send out bills at the much higher rate. If you paid anything more than the reasonable and customary fee, you're due a refund.

This could mean several hundred dollars coming back to you. Say, for example, that your insurance company pays for 80% of what is reasonable and customary. You received a bill of $475 for the procedure. You paid the whole amount up front, assuming the insurance company would reimburse you for 80% of that ($380), bringing your out of pocket cost down to $95.

But a call to your insurance company reveals the reasonable and customary charge is only $300. You overpaid, so you're owed a refund of $175 from the doctor's office. Your insurer will reimburse you for 80% of the $300 ($240), bringing your total cost down to $60 ($475 - $175 - $240 = **$60**).

So how do you get your money back?

Simple. Call the doctor's office and tell them you want back the $175 you overpaid. Since they never should have charged you the higher amount in the first place, you'll get it, along with the $240 from the insurance company. Those two phone calls will get you checks for a total of $415.

Incorrect bills like this add up over the course of a year. One set of parents were charged the standard fee of $80 for each of 50 allergy visits during a one year period for their son. The paid the 20% co-payment of $16 each time.

But the reasonable and customary charge for the allergy visits was only $24, which meant a co-payment of only $4.80. They had been overcharged $560 [$11.20 a visit times 50 weeks]. When they discovered the error, they received the refund of $560.

Look at every bill you paid this year, last year and the year before, and it's easy to see how you can receive refunds totaling thousands of dollars.

In the future, you'll check the reasonable and customary charges before you pay, so you won't be loaning doctors' offices money that really belongs to you.

Reasonable and customary charges apply to doctor visits, lab tests, medical treatment, hospital fees and dental costs. Ask your provider for the procedure code, then ask your insurer for the reasonable and customary fee. You can keep a list of codes and fees for basic procedures: office visits, x-rays, etc., and you won't have to call each time.

CHAPTER 8—GOING BACK AND COLLECTING THOUSANDS

Just because you overpaid last year doesn't mean you can't get that money back this year. You can go back one, three, and even five years and get refunds for medical overcharges.

If you paid the same bills your insurer did in the past, you can get reimbursed now, years after the fact. Look up the x-ray for your back problem from two years ago, for example, and compare it to the statement of benefits you received from your insurer. If you and your insurance company both paid for it, you can demand—and get—the lab to refund your money. They won't even argue with you about it, because they don't want any close inquiries into their double-billing practices. They'll just claim it was an error and send you a refund.

Do the same thing with old hospital bills. Did you pay the surgeon when the insurance company also sent him or her a check? Or maybe you paid it a second time in a lump sum hospital bill? Did you receive, and pay, separate bills for emergency room service and hospitalization then later discover the hospitalization bill also included the ER?

Look closely at claims your insurance company turned down. Go item by item with your old records, chapter by chapter with this book. Were procedures coded wrong, then underpaid or denied completely? Did your insurer claim your treatment or procedure wasn't medically necessary or not covered under your policy? Did they deem your emergency room visit not an emergency? Were the costs for treating your pre-existing condition denied when they should have been covered? Did they pay for fewer days of hospitalization than your doctor authorized? Did your hospital bill contain charges for treatments or tests you didn't receive?

Use the same system from the earlier chapters to go over your old bills. Chapter 6, for example, tells you more about reading through and challenging bills after you get home from the hospital. Chapter 5 details how you get ripped off by double-billing and lump sum bills. Chapter 7 explains how to pay the lower reasonable and customary charges for all your medical costs. Chapter 26 has the worksheet you will need to get your refunds. Even years later, you can get reimbursed for overcharges like these. The checks you receive can be significant.

You might encounter some resistance from medical offices and hospitals about pulling old bills, but a little insistence on your part will work wonders. Don't be intimidated if they tell you the old records are in storage or have been purged from the computer. By law, your medical records must be saved. Allow a week or two for the old records to be pulled, then call again. If the second phone call doesn't work, a letter, specifying exactly what you want, should do the trick.

Do this for both sides of the equation: the doctor and the lab, the hospital and the surgeon, the lab and the insurance company. Once you get the records, compare them. If you paid twice, to the practitioner and the hospital, or if you and your insurance company paid the same bill, you can get your money refunded. This works as well for errors in the bills as for double-billing, even denials of coverage, if you haven't passed the time limit for an appeal.

Use one of the sample letters in chapter 25, enclose copies of the old bills, along with your cancelled checks if you still have them, and you'll get your money refunded in the mail.

Getting reimbursed for old overpayments takes a little more persistence, but remember, the money that was overpaid belongs to you. Isn't that worth a little time?

CHAPTER 9—CAFETERIA PLANS:
NOT FOOD, BUT PRE-TAX SAVINGS PLANS

Did you know that most big companies, and many small ones, allow you to pay your medical costs in pre-tax dollars?

What this means is you can pay your medical expenses with the full value of your salary, before taxes are deducted.

Say you're in the 28% federal tax bracket. That means a thousand dollars of salary is only $720 in take home pay. You lose even more money to FICA (social security) and state taxes. Subtract those taxes, too, and you may be left with only $600, maybe much less.

But you don't have to lose that $400.

Best of all, this has nothing to do with complex forms or itemizing on your tax returns.

Cafeteria plans allow you to set aside a certain amount, designated by you, to pay for your medical costs, and you won't have to pay income taxes on those medical dollars.

Unlike insurance plans, cafeteria plan dollars can be used to pay for any medical expense, not only approved or covered costs. Any medical expense, including insurance premiums, office visits, hospitalization, dental, vision and psychotherapy, apply.

Here's how it works. You designate a certain amount to be taken out of each paycheck and held for you in a medical cafeteria account. Say you elect $25 a week, for a total of $1300 a year. Normally, after taxes, your take home pay from that $1300 would be only about $780. Divide that by 52 weeks, and your paycheck after the cafeteria deduction would be smaller by only $15 a week.

Without a cafeteria plan, you'd only have the $780 left to spend on medical care. With a cafeteria plan, you'll get $1300 of medical care for $780, or even less, depending on your tax bracket.

Whenever you have a medical expense that isn't reimbursed by your insurer, you submit the receipt to the cafeteria plan and get a check in the mail within a few weeks. It's that easy. There's no such thing as not medically necessary, not covered, deductibles, or reasonable and customary. You can submit anything that isn't paid by your insurance company: co-payments, office visits, hospitalization, prescription drugs, lab tests, dental work, glasses, physical therapy, counseling, costs before your deductible is met, even your part of the insurance premium.

You submit the receipt, the cafeteria plan sends you the check, and you come out way ahead. Look at how much money you'll save. You got reimbursed for $1300 worth of medical expenses, but if you hadn't signed up for the cafeteria plan, you would have taken home only $780 of that $1300, so you made a $520 profit!

The higher your medical bills are, the more money you'll make.

Most companies allow you to sign up when you're first hired or during their open enrollment period. You only commit for one year at a time. You can even change the amount if you have what's known as a qualifying event: a marriage, divorce, birth, adoption or death.

The only caution is that cafeteria plans are use it or lose it plans, so estimate your annual medical costs carefully. If you have money left over near the end of the year, you can always use it for your new glasses or that dental work you've been putting off. You must "pay" for the expenses during the year.

If you can't find a Cafeteria Plan in your employee benefits book, that may be because it's listed under another name. Cafeteria plans are also called Flexible Spending Accounts, Flex Benefits or 125 Plans. Ask your Human Resources office if you still can't find it. It's such a popular benefit, even many smaller firms are offering it.

CHAPTER 10—IF THEY CALL IT
THE WRONG THING,
YOU WON'T GET PAID

If your doctor's office tells the insurance company you just had an annual physical, not a medical problem, forget it, your insurer won't pay.

While regular check-ups make good medicine, most insurance companies still won't cover preventative care. You have to be sick to get coverage. If they call it or code it the wrong thing, you won't get the bill paid.

So if your doctor's office writes "annual exam" or "physical" on the claim form, your insurance company will try to deny payment for the charges—for the office visit and all the lab tests.

Often you go to the doctor with a real problem. But if your doctor didn't identify that on the form, your claim will be rejected.

To get your bills paid, you need to make sure your initial complaint is identified to the insurance company. It doesn't matter if it turned out to be nothing. As long as you had a reason for going in, even if your suspicions turned out to be wrong, your office visit and any tests you had should be covered.

If you went to the doctor because you're tired all the time, have headaches or have insomnia, the visit and accompanying tests should be covered to the extent of your policy.

Any time you went to see the doctor with a specific complaint, and the coverage gets turned down, ask the insurance company what the doctor listed as the problem. It doesn't matter what the diagnosis is, or even if the treatment is a lifestyle change, not medical treatment. If you went with a problem, the insurance company has to cover it.

Insurance companies are notorious for not wanting to cover gynecological care. If the policy reads that birth control prescriptions, which usually require doctor visits every six months, aren't covered, make sure your doctor doesn't list the wrong reason for your appointment. An annual check-up or a prescription refill may not be covered, but menstrual cramps are, as long as the office visit is coded correctly.

If your claim was turned down because the claim form or doctor's invoice didn't list a complaint, have the doctor resubmit it with the correct information. Call your doctor's office and tell them to code your stomachache, your sore throat, your insomnia on the form to identify that you went in with a specific medical complaint, not for a general check-up.

You're also covered if your condition isn't as bad as you thought it was. If you thought you broke your toe, but only bruised it, if your ankle was sprained, not broken, if your stomachache was due to stress, not an ulcer, make sure your original complaint, not just the diagnosis, gets listed on the insurance form. If there was a reasonable belief that you had a broken bone, you're entitled to an x-ray. The same goes for tests for ulcers, strep throats, etc. Part of diagnosis is ruling out, so if your doctor ordered tests, your insurer should be paying for them.

But your doctor's billing service may not have listed everything correctly. Remember, a wrong code means a wrong payment. In the medical billing industry, wrong usually means less. Even a blood cholesterol test can be coded in more than one way, so make sure to verify everything.

There are so many ways for your bills to be submitted wrong. Did they write down physical exam, not recurring headaches, gynecological exam instead of menstrual cramps? If so, have your doctor's office give you the form with the correct complaint, fax that to your insurance company, and get it paid for.

CHAPTER 11—GETTING IT COVERED AFTER YOU ARE TURNED DOWN BY YOUR INSURANCE COMPANY

Insurance companies are notorious for denying claims with a simple, "It was not medically necessary," or "We don't cover that."

You can say, "Yes, it was," and "Yes, you do," and get your bills paid.

To fight these types of vague excuses, first check your policy. Look at your summary of benefits, which highlights both what is covered and what you have to pay, like a $10 co-payment for an office visit or nothing on lab tests with a participating lab. There's a good chance you'll find the coverage you want listed right there. If not, read the actual policy itself, which is more detailed and more specific.

Once you find that your test or treatment is covered, you can solve the problem with a phone call or letter to the insurance company. Call first. If they pay the claim, fine. If they resist, photocopy the page that says they really do cover the item, and fax it to them with a brief letter. (Chapter 25 has a sample letter.) You'll get the bill paid.

Fighting denials of "not medically necessary," aren't much harder. Remember, you can challenge every decision made by the healthcare industry. If, for example, your doctor decided your mammography or cholesterol test was medically necessary, but your insurance company disagreed, you can fight the decision and win.

Not medically necessary is often an excuse used by insurance companies when they don't want to pay for expensive treatment. They'll even use it to avoid paying for relatively inexpensive tests. Even if the test cost only $50, multiply that by thousands of rejected claims, and it equals a lot of extra money for them.

Insurance companies have tables that indicate how often, and at what age, people are covered for routine exams and tests. Whether it's a mammogram or a prostate exam, the chart usually says people can't get coverage until a specific age or not more often than every two or five years. If your doctor recommends the exam or the test outside of those limits, you may find yourself with a bill.

Medical guidelines for diagnostic tests on common and serious illnesses change all the time. But the guidelines list risk averages for the general population, not your particular situation. If you have a family history of colon cancer, a tendency toward diabetes or a high likelihood of cholesterol problems, you legitimately need the tests earlier and more often.

Maybe your test from last year came back in the high normal range—not dangerous, but worth monitoring. Or three of your uncles had diabetes. Your doctor, however, didn't indicate that to the insurance company. You can get the bill covered by having your doctor explain the prior test results, or your family history, which should have been done in the first place.

While your insurance company may tell you that the treatment, "was not medically necessary," insurance companies aren't doctors. If your doctor prescribed the treatment, you can usually get the bill covered. Often, the policy itself clearly states that they cover outside the limits under specific circumstances. Read through your policy to find what exceptions apply in your case. It may be clearly spelled out.

There also isn't a single way to treat a particular condition. Ulcers, for example, can be treated in a variety of different ways—from lifestyle changes to medication to surgery. Your doctor may use the treatment that is the most effective for you, not the one that is the cheapest. So when your insurance company turns you down, your doctor's office should call the insurance company to straighten it out, and you should get the coverage approved. If a phone call doesn't work, a letter will.

Insurance companies also try to get out of paying for care by specialists. One way they try to do that is by claiming the care wasn't necessary or there is no record of a referral by your primary care physician. Both of these problems can be solved by following the simple guidelines in chapter 13.

Insurance companies often turn down coverage for procedures that are experimental. But their information may be out of date. A man in New York needed surgery to repair a knee he had injured jogging. The doctor filed the correct paperwork for prior approval, but the insurance company turned the request down, claiming the new surgical procedure was still experimental.

The patient filed an appeal, showed that the procedure had been approved by the FDA, and got his surgery paid for.

The most important things to know are: what your policy covers, and never take no for an answer. If you get a denial from your insurer that says, "not medically necessary," call your doctor's office so you can explain why it was. If your insurer tells you a particular treatment or exam isn't covered, ask them why. Once you know that, you'll know how to challenge it.

So when your insurance company sends you a statement saying, "not covered," you can write them back and get yourself a check.

CHAPTER 12—EMERGENCY ROOM SCARES

Emergency room treatment is notoriously expensive, so many insurers try to deny coverage for it.

Patients are often told their emergency room visit wasn't really an emergency, so they get stuck with a bill for hundreds or thousands of dollars instead of a nominal co-payment.

Emergency room tests and treatment run much higher than the same care in a doctor's office or an outpatient lab; it's not unusual for something as simple as an x-ray to be three or four times as expensive as the same test outside of the hospital. Ruling out a fractured wrist in the ER can easily cost over $500, while a single x-ray would cost way under a $100 in your doctor's office. No wonder they do not want to pay for it.

That's why you want to make sure your emergency care is covered as emergency care, even if your illness or injury wasn't as bad as you thought it was.

If your chest pain turned out to be heartburn, not a heart attack, it doesn't mean you are responsible for a big bill. The same thing holds if your twisted ankle turned out to be a sprain, not a fracture. The law requires that if a person reasonably believes he or she has a serious medical problem, or is in significant pain, an emergency room visit is warranted, and the insurance company must cover it. While a cold won't be covered, severe stomach pain will.

Even if your insurance policy requires prior authorization for care, that doesn't apply to emergencies. The 1996 Kennedy-Kassenbaum law, which created sweeping new regulations for health insurance coverage, mandates that individuals must have access to emergency care, without prior authorization, in any situation that a "prudent lay person" would regard as an emergency.

While insurance companies may require prior approval for non-emergency surgery, specialist referrals and most lab tests, tests and treatments for emergencies are different. The new law prevents them from denying payment for emergency care. So while they can require advance approval for a hernia operation, they can't for an appendix that is about to burst. Your insurer may try to deny payment, but you don't have to let them get away with it.

If you paid an emergency room bill that was denied because your insurance company claimed it wasn't an emergency, you can get your money refunded. Just fill in the blanks in the letter in chapter 25. A check should follow within a couple of weeks.

But do be careful about returning to the emergency room. Even if the ER doctor told you to come back in a couple of days, your insurance company will consider that follow-up care and deny your claim. Instead, call your regular doctor and either make an appointment, or get a referral to a specialist, if that's what you need.

CHAPTER 13—REFERRALS:
GET THAT SPECIALIST PAID FOR

Medical charges, particularly physical therapy and lab tests, are routinely denied because they require prior written authorization from your doctor on most health insurance plans.

If the insurance company doesn't have the authorization from your doctor, get that and the charges will be covered. Call you doctor's office, get a copy of the authorization, and send it on to your insurance company, preferably by fax. It's quicker than the mail, and the sooner they get it, the sooner your coverage gets approved.

The same thing stands for seeing a specialist. Most plans, including HMOs, PPOs and POS plans, require a referral from your primary care doctor. If your doctor's office didn't do the paperwork properly, your insurance company won't pay for it. If this happened to you, call the doctor's office to get the referral and send it yourself to the insurance company. That way you'll make sure it gets done and gets done right away. When your insurance company receives the referral, your visit to the specialist, which can cost a couple of hundred dollars, will be covered to the extent of your policy.

Another common billing error is when patients are overcharged for seeing a doctor within the insurance network of specialists. Even though her doctor referred her, one woman was charged $330 by her insurance company for seeing a specialist the insurance company claimed was not in their physician's network. The specialist really was within the network, so she challenged the bill and received a complete refund.

The problem happened because it took months, as it often does, for the specialist to be entered into the system. So when your insurer says no, and you know the answer is supposed to be yes, be persistent. Your health insurance is expensive enough; you want to make sure you get your full benefits.

How often has your doctor referred you to a specialist, within your plan's network, and your insurance company still told you the referral wasn't covered? The solution may be as simple as having your doctor explain the referral.

A woman in her late thirties was sent to an ophthalmologist instead of an optometrist because of a family history of glaucoma. The insurance company didn't cover ophthalmologists for routine annual exams, so only after the woman's primary care physician wrote "family history" on the referral form was the office visit covered. The patient paid a $10 co-payment, not the full fee for a specialist, which could have been several hundred dollars.

If your insurer resists paying, asking your doctor's office for a letter that explains your condition and why specialist care is needed should do the trick.

Referrals often take three to five days to get into the system, so unless your situation is an emergency, make the appointment for a week or two in the future, and you just may solve the problem in advance. If you can't wait that long, make sure to get a copy of the referral from your doctor's office. The date on the written referral will be your proof if you need to challenge the insurance company's denial of coverage.

Always make sure you understand what has to be approved in advance and what the limitations are. Physical therapy referrals, for example, are usually covered for a specified number of visits (like three times a week for four weeks). The therapist then needs to issue a progress report and your doctor and insurance company can authorize a continued treatment referral.

You have the right to see a specialist when your condition requires it. So whether you need an orthopedist, an internist or a cancer doctor, get that referral and you'll get it covered.

But some specialists don't require a referral. Most plans allow a self-referral for a "well-woman exam" once a year, which includes a pap smear and a breast exam.

If you live in an area like Florida, California or Arizona with a high rate of skin cancer, you may be allowed an annual visit to a dermatologist on your own. But doctors and insurance companies routinely send out bills anyway. So if you or someone in your family went for a covered self-referral and got billed anyway, call your insurance company, remind them of the policy, and you'll get the charges removed.

CHAPTER 14—SECOND OPINIONS: YOU'RE ENTITLED

Whenever you're diagnosed with a serious condition, you're entitled to a second opinion. Whether it's your primary care doctor or a specialist who recommends a hip replacement, ulcer treatment, back surgery, chemotherapy, you have the right to insurance coverage for a second opinion from another doctor.

That means you get to see two specialists, even if your primary care doctor made the initial diagnosis. After you discuss your condition and treatment options with the first specialist, your insurer must pay, to the extent of your policy, for a consultation with a second one. Whether it's a disease or an injury, you're covered.

Medical diagnosis and treatment is not an exact science. While an infection can be easily confirmed with a simple lab test, diseases like Chronic Fatigue Syndrome and Multiple Sclerosis are not as easy to diagnose. You not only want a second opinion on the treatment, you want a second opinion on the diagnosis itself.

Even after your condition is clearly diagnosed, you may have several options: surgery or drugs, drugs or a lifestyle change, monitoring or treatment.

Many, many conditions have several treatment opinion. Cancer, most obviously, can be treated with drugs (chemotherapy), radiation or surgery, or even a combination of the three. Even within each of these options, there are choices. Breast cancer, for example, can be treated surgically with a lumpectomy, a radical mastectomy or a simple (less drastic) mastectomy, with or without accompanying radiation and/or chemotherapy.

With cancer and other diseases, there is also a constant influx of experimental and new procedures. Your doctor may not be up to date on all of the options.

Some options may have serious consequences or side effects and two experts are better than one. Or maybe you just need to hear the same thing from two people for peace of mind.

Whether its confirmation you need or help evaluating when there's no clear, best choice, it makes sense to get another expert opinion. After all, if you were remodeling your house, you'd be advised to get bids from more than one contractor. Why should you do any less where your health is concerned?

The law agrees, and insurers are required to cover the costs of second opinions just like they cover first opinions. If you're in an HMO, you'll have to stay within your network, if another specialist is available. In a PPO, you may get more choice. No matter what type of plan you have, even one you pay for yourself, or one sponsored by the government, like Medicare, the law guarantees that you get to consult with another physician, and your insurer has to pay.

CHAPTER 15—ON THE ROAD: GETTING COVERAGE WHEN YOU TRAVEL

Most insurance companies have coverage for treatment on the road for emergencies—anything from a throat infection to a heart attack. But you may find yourself with a bill anyway.

The reason may be the same double-billing we discussed in chapter 5.

A traveler who got an ear infection on a road trip called her insurance company at their toll free number, within 24 hours, as required by the policy, and they set up an appointment for her at a local clinic, with no co-payment, no charges. She was examined, received her antibiotics and was on her way.

But a month later, she received a bill in the mail from the clinic. Clinics and labs all over the country routinely send bills to both patients and their insurance companies. Just like the lab and the doctor you go to in your own city, they don't care who they get paid from; they just want to get paid. If both parties pay, then they get paid twice, and they don't complain about that.

If you've already paid a bill, find out if your insurance company did, too. If so, you can demand, and get, a refund. In the traveler's case, she called her insurance company, and they told her the bill was in the process of being paid, so she didn't have to.

Most insurance policies have provisions if you get sick or injured while travelling—whether for business or for pleasure. You can often get the medical bills covered, even if you went outside of your network. Look at your policy and see if it covers all medical care or only emergencies when you're on the road and far away from your network. You should be covered, for emergencies at least, minus any co-payment or deductible, as long as you're a certain number of miles away from home. Remember, emergency care doesn't only mean life or death situations like a heart attack. It also covers routine problems like infections and muscle sprains that need immediate attention.

You may not always need advance authorization for treatment on the road, even if your policy requires it. While insurance companies may require prior approval for treating a sprained ankle or a strep throat, a serious emergency is different.

Remember the "prudent lay person standard" from chapter 12: individuals must have access to emergency care, without prior authorization, in any situation that a prudent lay person would regard as an emergency.

So if your insurance company refused to reimburse you for your bill because you didn't call them for permission first, you can cite this law and get them to send you a check.

The most important thing to know is to always keep your receipts. If you got medical treatment on a cruise ship or had to see the hotel doctor in a foreign country, you really didn't have any other choice. And you certainly couldn't call your insurance company with any ease.

When you get home from your trip, call your insurance company to find out how to submit your claim, then send a letter explaining the circumstances, along with the receipts for your medical care. It makes no difference if you have an individual policy, one from work or a plan that covers you in retirement. They may try to deny your claim at first, but that doesn't mean you'll let them get away with it. If you're right, a few phone calls or letters should get your bills paid.

Remember the cardinal rule: read your insurance policy to see what it covers, be aware of the laws explained in this book that guarantee you medical care and coverage, and fight anything you disagree with.

As any two year old knows, no doesn't always mean no. Keep pushing, and you'll get your care paid for.

CHAPTER 16—DRIVE-THROUGH CHILDBIRTH AND OTHER STUNTS THEY CAN'T GET AWAY WITH ANYMORE

The days when your insurance company could determine a short hospital stay for a lengthy illness are coming to an end. Until recently, insurers could deny extra nights in the hospital, regardless of the patient's health or the doctor's recommendations, even for people undergoing major surgery or physically traumatic events.

The biggest scandal was insurance companies limiting coverage for certain procedures to 23 hours, saving thousand of dollars on an overnight hospital stay. Even when doctors determined that patients required longer hospitalizations for observation or medical care, insurance companies refused to pay.

Insurers based their decisions on average recuperation times. But the reasoning is so flawed that anyone with basic math skills can figure it out. If, on average, a person needs three days to recover from a particular illness or procedure, that means some people need one day and some people need five.

Most frequently, insurers wouldn't allow women to stay in the hospital overnight after childbirth or allow mastectomy patients enough days in the hospital to recover, causing healthcare advocates and legislators to name them "drive-through procedures."

Federal and state laws are changing to insure not only care, but coverage. Congress recently passed a law banning "Drive-through Childbirth," so if your insurance company doesn't want to pay for your overnight hospital stay after giving birth, that's too bad. They have to pay the bill.

Remember you must have your primary care provider check you into the hospital in certain states to obtain full coverage for childbirth.

In 1996, President Clinton signed "The Newborns' and Mothers' Protection Act," a law guaranteeing women and their infants a 48 hour stay after childbirth for a normal delivery and 96 hours (4 days) after a cesarean section.

Before the law, women were being forced to leave the hospital as soon as eight hours after giving birth. This caused problems not only for new mothers, but the babies. Common problems with infants and new mothers that can be easily recognized and treated within a hospital setting include brain damage from untreated jaundice and dehydration from breast feeding problems. Several babies died before the law went into effect.

Now that the law is in effect, insurers must pay for the two or four day stays after delivery. The regulations went into effect in 1998, so if your insurer denied coverage after that time, you can get your money refunded. Chapter 8 will show you how to go back and get a refund for an old claim they should have paid in the first place.

The Women's Health and Cancer Rights Act of 1998, which went into effect on January 1, 1999, expanded coverage for women who undergo mastectomies.

The law guarantees that insurers in all fifty states cover reconstructive surgery after mastectomies. In the past, insurance companies could deny the reconstruction by deeming it cosmetic surgery or "not medically necessary." With the new law, all women with insured, self-insured plans and HMOs provided by private and governmental employers are guaranteed the reconstructive surgery.

Some states have even stricter laws. It's not hard to find out what they are. If the federal law guarantees you a 36 hour stay for a particular medical event, but the state insists on 48 hours, you get the 48 hours and your insurer has to pay for it.

States may even guarantee the doctor's right to determine a hospital stay of any length. Some states, like Connecticut, passed laws in the past few years that, "prohibit managed care organizations from limiting hospital stays following a mastectomy to any period of time less than that determined by the physician in consultation with the patient." Illinois and Montana offer similar protection. The end result for you? Whatever the doctor says you need, they have to pay for.

Now that you're aware of these new laws, you won't allow your health insurance company to play doctor with you any longer.

Usually a phone call citing the new law will get your hospital bill paid. If that doesn't work, use the sample letter in chapter 25.

CHAPTER 17—KNOW THE TESTS YOU ARE ENTITLED TO EITHER FREE OR CHEAP

New laws require that patients have the right to diagnostic tests when they are medically necessary, not only at arbitrary limits set by insurers.

So if your insurer tries to deny coverage for a mammogram when your aunt had breast cancer, a blood cholesterol test when you have a family history of heart disease, a PSA test when your uncles had prostate problems, you can get them to cover it.

Federal laws guarantee specific protections, but state laws often provide even better coverage. You don't have to search through arcane government files to find out what you're entitled to, either. The guarantees are usually listed right in your membership handbook.

Say your doctor recommends a mammogram, fills out the proper referral form, you get the mammogram, but your insurance company denies payment, claiming they don't cover the test because you're too young.

Well, they can't get away with it.

Florida, for example, insists that insurers pay for mammograms on female patients every year, or more often, if any of these risk factors are present, even if she doesn't have a single symptom:

-   the patient has a family history of breast cancer;
-   the patient didn't give birth to a child before 30;
-   the patient is over 50.

Other states have similar laws. So if your insurance company tries to deny your claim, all you have to do is look up the coverage, call or write, and they'll cancel the charge. You'll be referring to the guidelines in their book, and they can't fight that.

Tests for cholesterol levels, blood sugar, prostate problems, colon cancer and the like also can't be denied just because your age doesn't match the one on a chart. If your doctor has a medical reason to test or monitor you, the insurance company has to pay for it. It's usually as simple as faxing a letter or the treatment form you get from your doctor to the insurance company.

Make sure your doctor knows about your family history, and make sure he or she writes it down. If there is breast cancer, diabetes or high cholesterol in your family, tests can be authorized at a younger age or more frequently.

Most diseases are cheaper to treat in the early stages, so insurance companies want to catch them early. Get it coded correctly, and you'll not only get medical care, you'll get it paid for.

CHAPTER 18—PRE-EXISTING CONDITIONS: THE LAW THAT GIVES YOU COVERAGE

Insurance companies used to be able to deny coverage for pre-existing conditions, but they can't do that anymore.

In the past, you could lose coverage for any pre-existing conditions when you changed insurance plans because of a new job. Whether you suffer from a minor but chronic problem like tendonitis, or a more serious condition like diabetes, multiple sclerosis, cancer or AIDS, your insurer has to provide coverage within 12 months, or even less. Often, there won't be any waiting period at all.

Most people get their pre-existing conditions covered immediately. Here's how it works: as long as you were insured for at least 12 months, and didn't have a break in coverage for more than 62 days, your new insurer has to pay for your pre-existing condition. And the waiting period at your new job isn't even considered a break in coverage.

If you had insurance for less than a year before switching insurers, you still get a break. Say, for example, you were insured for the previous nine months. You only need three more months on your new policy to hit the twelve month mark. At the end of those three months, your pre-existing condition is covered completely.

So you can get your diabetes, your heart condition, your ulcer treated without any extra costs. The new law guarantees that your pre-existing condition gets covered with the same co-payments or deductibles as any new illness or injury.

Your insurer may try to deny coverage for your condition, but you can fight back with a new law. The Health Insurance Portability and Accountability Act of 1996, also known as the Kennedy-Kassenbaum law, guarantees coverage when you switch insurers.

The law mandates that pre-existing conditions cannot be excluded for longer than 12 months on new policies. Even better, this applies only to conditions treated or diagnosed within the six months before you enrolled in the insurance plan, so if your back problem from four years ago flares up again, you get your medical costs covered.

While your new insurer may try to deny your claim because you already suffered from a medical condition, you won't let them get away with it. As long as you had continuous insurance coverage for the past 12 months, they have to pay.

If they try to turn you down, the form letter in chapter 25 will get your condition covered and your bills paid.

It's all very simple. Be insured for 12 months, and you're covered, even for serious conditions.

Remember this for the future: if you switch jobs, take advantage of COBRA (explained in chapter 22) or some other form of health insurance. As long as you're not without health insurance for more than 62 days, they can't deny coverage for your pre-existing conditions. Keep your receipts, and the letter of continuous coverage your old insurer sent you when you left the plan. As long as you have documentation that you were covered, you'll get your bills paid.

CHAPTER 19—ANNUAL LIMITS: YOU DON'T HAVE TO PAY ANY MORE

You may not have to make co-payments all year long. While five or ten dollars may not seem like a lot of money, it's in addition to your monthly insurance premiums and it adds up quickly. And some co-payments, like for therapy, hospitalization or emergency room care, could be pretty high. Deductibles for your medical care also have limits. If you meet these before the end of the year, you will not have to pay anymore.

Insurance plans, whether HMOs that charge nominal co-payments for office visits, lab tests and hospitalization, or PPOs that pay a percentage of the costs after a certain deductible is met, all have annual limits on how much you have to pay. These are called annual out-of-pocket maximums. They can be reached by individual members or a family as a whole, so if one person has high medical bills, the whole family saves.

Once the family reaches the level, nobody has to pay any more for the rest of the year.

Your insurance company won't necessarily tell you you've reached the annual out-of-pocket limit, so it's up to you to keep accurate records and let them know when the burden of payment shifts to them.

The limits work like this. In an HMO, you have co-payments for doctor visits, specialist referrals, hospitalization, emergency room care and therapy. What plans don't emphasize is that you don't have to keep making the co-payments all year long. Once you hit the annual maximum, your insurance covers the rest.

Look on your detailed benefit summary for the specifics. The detailed benefit summary is the list that clearly spells out what your coverage is and what you have to pay. If you can't find the summary, call your insurance company and have them send you another copy. They should do that without a problem.

Most major HMO/POS/PPO plans have maximum annual co-payments of $1,500 per person or $3,000 per family in any calendar year. Just like deductibles, dollar amounts on annual maximums vary from one plan to the next, but your plan should have something similar. Once you reach those limits, you don't have to pay a cent more. Your insurer is obligated to cover the rest.

PPOs function in much the same way. Again, look at your detailed benefit summary to find out how much your annual out-of-pocket maximum is, per person and per family. If it's $2,000 per person or $5,000 per family, that can be covered with a brief hospitalization or a series of tests or treatments for one or two illnesses or injuries.

PPOs also have deductible maximums that can save you money, even if you don't reach your out-of-pocket limit. Your policy will pay a certain amount, like 80% of what is reasonable and customary, after the deductible is met. So if your deductible is $250 per person or $750 per family, once you've paid the $750 for any combination of people, you've met the deductible. After that, you only pay anything beyond the 80% of reasonable and customary, up to your annual out-of-pocket limit. And chapter 7 will make sure you don't get charged more than the reasonable and customary fees.

To make sure you're not writing checks in November when your obligation ended in May, keep receipts for all your medical costs. Add them up, and when you reach the annual out-of-pocket limit, you can stop paying for the year.

CHAPTER 20—MEDICARE:
DON'T LET THE GOVERNMENT CHEAT YOU

Insurance is insurance. At least as far as your benefits are concerned.

If you are covered by Medicare, you still have the same rights concerning the right to treatment and the right to get it paid for.

Many people think of Medicare as government welfare and are just grateful for whatever coverage they get. But that's not the case. You paid into the system for decades through payroll deductions. And since you paid the premiums, you have the right to fight for your benefits.

Like other insurance plans, Medicare has coverage schedules, participating medical care providers and an appeals process. Getting your coverage, and getting your coverage paid for, is no different with Medicare than with a private insurer. The process is the same, it just may take a little bit longer. Expect the government to take a little longer, but expect them to pay.

If Medicare rejects the bill because your procedure was coded incorrectly or they lost the paperwork on your referral to the specialist, follow the same steps as you would for an employment or individual policy. Look up the rules, call them up, explain where they went wrong, and get your money back or get the doctor or the hospital paid for.

A Medicare HMO requires that you get all of your medical care within the network. If you get sick or injured when you're travelling, that may not be possible. But that may not stop the HMO from trying to deny your claim. That also doesn't have to stop you from challenging their decision. Remember what you learned in chapter 12: you have the right to seek treatment for a perceived medical emergency, without prior approval, and your insurance company must pay for it.

If you also have a supplemental policy, either through Medicare or as a pension benefit, you'll need to check and compare the coverage for both policies. Your doctor visit, for example, may be covered by Medicare, but your prescriptions may be covered by the supplemental policy. So look at your summary notice (the Medicare statement that list what physicians, hospitals and labs are billing Medicare for their services). Make sure all dates and procedures are correct. Then compare it with any statement you get from your supplemental insurer. A lot of problems can be solved with this simple step.

Remember, there are two types of problems in getting your medical care paid for:

- denial of coverage;
- and errors.

Determine if Medicare just doesn't want to pay for your care or if they made a mistake. If they don't want to pay, identify why—they thought your test was unnecessary, they still had your treatment listed as experimental after it was approved by the FDA—and then you'll know how to fight it. If they made an error, determine what kind—they got the procedure code wrong, they don't have the referral on file—and you can quickly solve the problem. Use the same information and processes explained in the earlier chapters to get your money back.

With Medicare, you can appeal any charge over $100. The process is explained on the back of your Medicare statement.

But most of the problems in getting Medicare to pay for your medical costs are no different than getting your private insurance company to pay. Mistakes are number one, so find the errors and you'll solve the problems. If they don't believe the care was necessary, a letter from your doctor just may do the trick. The key is not to give up. After all, you worked hard all these years to earn your coverage. Why not enjoy your benefits now?

CHAPTER 21—THE LAW GUARANTEES IT, EVEN WHEN YOUR DOCTOR LEAVES THE PLAN

These days, doctors are constantly joining and leaving insurance plans, but laws exist that allow you to continue treatment with your doctor for existing conditions.

This is particularly important if you're being treated for something serious like cancer or a heart condition. But if you're pregnant, have an ulcer or are healing from a torn shoulder, you can still probably finish your treatment not only if your doctor left the plan, but even if your insurance company was switched by your employer.

So if you're billed for out of network service or charged for a doctor who doesn't participate in the plan anymore, you can get the bills covered in many instances.

The law isn't very specific, so you may have to fight for your coverage. The general rule is that your insurer has to provide coverage for you to keeping going to the same doctor, "to avoid interruption of care."

If you are recovering from surgery, have a problem pregnancy or are undergoing continuing treatment for an injury or illness, you should be able to get your insurer to pay your old doctor.

First, call your insurer and explain your particular situation, detailing how long your doctor has been treating you for this problem, how much longer the treatment is expected to continue and why a change in physicians would be detrimental to your health. Since the standard is "avoiding interruption of care," if there is a wait for appointments with the new physician, or it will take a while for the new doctor to get up to speed because your condition is complicated, stress that.

If your insurance company resists, have your doctor write a letter explaining why switching doctors at this point in your medical care would not be in your best interest. Again, make sure the letter is as specific as possible. The insurance company needs a reason to say yes. If the illness or injury only needs treatment for a finite period of time, that should be stressed. Your insurer may be reluctant to approve out-of-network coverage for a lifetime of monitoring a heart murmur, but probably won't resist three weeks of follow-up care after pacemaker surgery.

In many cases, you'll get the medical care paid for. But if you don't, you haven't run out of options. Chapter 24 will take you through the appeals process. Do pay strict attention to dates if you go this route, because appeals have to be filed within a specific timeframe.

With the rules in this area so vague, an appeal may get you the care you need with the doctor of your choice.

It may take a bit of work, but these steps should get your treatment covered, even though your doctor left the plan.

CHAPTER 22—COBRA: KEEP YOUR INSURANCE, EVEN WHEN YOU LEAVE YOUR JOB

Just because you leave your job don't mean you have to leave your health insurance behind. Even if you quit, you're entitled to continue on your employer's health insurance plan for at least 18 months.

A law called COBRA (Consolidated Omnibus Budget Reconciliation Act), guarantees that most people can keep their health coverage for 18 months after they leave their jobs. While your employer may have paid all or part of your health insurance premiums as one of your benefits, with COBRA, you will be required to pay the premiums yourself, but you are guaranteed the right to purchase the insurance.

This is particularly important if you have any pre-existing conditions. While chapter 18 discusses this in greater detail, if you have continuous health insurance for at least 12 months, a new insurer cannot deny coverage for your pre-existing conditions. A break of a few months in insurance coverage could mean that your new insurer, whether it's an individual policy you purchase yourself or one you get with your new job, wouldn't cover any of the expenses for your condition—anything from asthma to a heart condition—for a full year.

Get COBRA and that won't happen. Not to you and not to your family.

If you've been insured for less than the 12 months, it's even more important. Not only can you and your family continue to get covered for any existing medical problems, but COBRA will help you reach the all important 12 month line so you won't have any pre-existing limitations when you get new insurance from your new job.

You're entitled to COBRA if your former employer has 20 or more employees (unless you were fired for gross misconduct or the company no longer offers health insurance). By law, your former employer must notify you of your COBRA rights. You have 60 days to decide whether or not to purchase the coverage. COBRA also allows you to add new family members later on if you get married, have a baby or adopt a child.

Under ordinary circumstances, you can purchase the coverage for up to 18 months. But special situations may allow you to purchase the coverage for an even longer period of time.

If you, or anyone in your family is disabled, your whole family is entitled to COBRA for 29 months. This applies even if someone becomes disabled after you leave your job, as long as it's within the first 60 days of COBRA coverage. Even if the disabled individual is a child, the entire family can extend COBRA coverage from the 18 to 29 months. In the case of death or divorce, spouses and dependents are entitled to 36 months of COBRA insurance.

So, whether you quit your job, got laid off or were fired, you can keep your health insurance. Health insurance premiums can be difficult when you don't have a paycheck, but they're a lot smaller than hospital bills.

CHAPTER 23—DOES YOUR DENTAL BILL HURT MORE THAN YOUR ROOT CANAL?

Because most people are so afraid of dental work, they're just grateful for the relief of pain and don't even bother to question the bills that come in the mail.

Even if you have dental insurance, the bills can be hefty. For anything other than a routine cleaning or filling of a cavity, many plans offer just a small discount, maybe 20% or 25% off the regular rates.

But dental bills contain the same types of errors as doctor and hospital bills, so treat them the same way.

For example, plans without a specific fee schedule offer discounts off lower, contracted rates, called reasonable and customary rates, which are explained in much greater detail in chapter 7. These rates are much lower than the standard ones your dentist charges, so whenever you get a bill, first make sure you were billed at the lower rate. Then make sure that the discount was applied and make sure the percentage was current.

Say your dentist's office billed you $125 for the procedure, minus the 20% discount, leaving you with a balance owed of $100. But if the reasonable and customary rate is $75, minus your 20% discount, you only owe $60. If you paid the bill at the dentist's office, they owe you a $40 refund.

Here's what to do to uncover and recover in cases like this:
- ask your dentist's office for the procedure code;
- call your insurer and ask what the reasonable and customary rate for the procedure is;
- subtract your discount;
- if you paid more than you were supposed to, call your dentist's office and tell them they overcharged you.

You should get it corrected with a phone call. Occasionally, you may have to send a letter, but just like with hospitals and labs, they don't want anyone to look too closely at their billing practices, so you should get your bill reduced, or your money refunded, promptly.

Miscoding of procedures is just as prevalent in dental offices as in doctor's offices. How many people, for example, know that there are half a dozen codes for tooth extractions? If the wrong one was listed for you, you'll get a bill you don't deserve. You don't want to get reimbursed only $50 for a $200 procedure just because someone typed the wrong number in the computer.

Or things may have gotten more complex during the procedure, but the billing department still listed the original code. The more complicated the procedure, the higher the coverage. If this happened to you, call the insurance company, ask what the code means—do they have it down as a simple extraction when you actually had anesthesia and stitches?—then have your dentist's office correct it.

Most small dental practices do their billing in-house. The person who does the billing may also make appointments and greet patients when they come in the door. This increases the chance for errors.

All cavities, for example, are not the same. Teeth have five surfaces: the four sides and the top. Filling are charged according to the number of sides affected. The more sides affected, the higher the bill.

If your insurance statement shows a lower reimbursement than you expected, call your dentist's office and ask them to compare the billing statement with your chart. If the computer says it was a two surface filling, but the chart says three, you can have it corrected, and get the higher reimbursement from your insurance company.

If a corner of your tooth chips off, the repair, called an incisal angle, will cost as much as a four surface filling. You want to make sure it was coded that way, or you won't get the full coverage.

Always go to the chart to check for errors. Busy practices may resist, but it's your money, and they'll do it if you insist. After all, if it wasn't coded correctly, it's money out of your pocket.

Not all errors happen during the billing process. Insurance companies also make mistakes or deny coverage for no good reason. Frequently, your dentist's office does use the correct code for the procedure you received, but your insurer tries to pay a lower benefit. They call this "applying an alternative benefit."

Say you hadn't been to a dentist for a number of years. You get an exam and x-rays, which are covered correctly. But since you haven't had a cleaning for five years, instead of the regular cleaning and polishing, which may take the hygienist twenty or thirty minutes, you need a procedure to remove the five years of plaque. Since that takes over an hour, the charge is much higher.

But when your statement comes back from your insurance company, it turns out they only paid the fee for a regular cleaning, and they want you to pay the rest.

Ask the dental hygienist for a letter explaining the need for the more extensive procedure, and you should it covered.

Most dentists want payment at the time of treatment, but just because you paid a bill when you were afraid or in pain, doesn't mean you can't challenge it later. Look at the invoice days, weeks or months later. Verify the procedure code. Call your insurance company to find out what the correct contracted rate for the procedure was and how much the discount should have been.

If you were overcharged, call your dentist's office armed with the information from your insurance company, and you'll get that overpayment refunded to you.

Just like with doctor's offices, labs and hospitals, start with a phone call. If that doesn't get your bill reduced or your money refunded, follow it up with a faxed or mailed letter. Nobody wants a close examination of their billing practices, so refunds are pretty easy to get.

Treat your dental bills no differently than your doctor and hospital bills. Make sure the charges are itemized, check for mistakes from the dental office, the billing department and the insurer, and contest anything you don't agree with. Just because you lost a tooth doesn't mean you have to lose your money.

CHAPTER 24—THE APPEALS PROCESS: GETTING PAID AFTER THEY SAY NO

When your insurance company turns down your request for coverage, that's not the final word. You have the legal right to appeal, and it won't cost you anything but a couple of cents in postage.

Every insurance company has a specific appeals process that is detailed in your policy. If you can't find it, call and have another copy sent to you, but be very conscious of dates. Policies usually require that you file your appeal within a specific timeframe, so make sure to send the initial form or letter before that date. Even if your medical care provider is writing on your behalf, make sure you appeal the decision in writing or you may lose your right to appeal at all.

You can appeal a decision no matter who your insurer is. Whether you're covered by a private plan or government insurance like Medicare, you can appeal any decision you disagree with. Just because someone else, like your employer or the government, is paying for your insurance doesn't mean you don't have the right to full benefits.

No matter what your policy is, your appeal must be in writing. It must also be directed to a specific person or department. So before you send the letter, get a name or department at your insurance company and a mailing address or fax number. Getting your appeal in the right hands in the first place not only makes things happen faster, it's also easier to follow up in the future if you know who to contact.

When making an appeal, first take a look at why the coverage was denied. If you don't understand, call your insurance company and ask for an explanation.

If they turned you down because of an error—miscoding of a procedure, a missing referral form, denying tests or treatment that really are covered—follow the recommended steps in the appropriate chapter earlier in the book.

If the insurance company disagrees with the medical necessity of your test or treatment, enlist the help of your physician. A letter from him or her explaining your condition and why a particular test or treatment was given can go a long way to getting your medical care paid for. If the chosen treatment had fewer side effects or was less invasive, that gives a solid medical reason for the choice.

While the word "appeal" may be scary, an appeal is just an extension of everything that's covered in this book: determine why coverage was denied, call or write to challenge the denial, and hopefully, get your medical care paid for.

If the written appeal doesn't got the results you want, you can often request a formal hearing. Your policy will explain the specific procedure and the timeline you need to follow. If your coverage was turned down because the procedure was deemed experimental, or the amount disputed is very high, you may have to go this route. But this can mean the coverage you deserve and the medical treatment you need.

The cost: a couple of stamps and a couple of hours.

The risk: none.

The reward: money in your pocket.

The worst they can do is say no, and they've already done that. Why not try to get them to say yes?

CHAPTER 25—OBTAINING REFUNDS WHEN THE SYSTEM TURNS YOU DOWN: VERY IMPORTANT LETTERS YOU CAN USE

In order to get a refund when your claim is denied, you need to know why the system turned you down in the first place.

First, take a look at why coverage was denied. Is the referral form from your doctor missing? Was your treatment coded incorrectly? Does your insurer claim that your diagnostic test isn't covered because you're too young to need it?

If you don't know why coverage was denied, call your insurance company and ask. Have them explain every single code, every reason for every denial of coverage.

Once you have this information, you'll know how to proceed.

Often, you can get assistance from your doctor's office. A letter from your doctor will help when you were turned down because of an error in coding or because your insurer deemed the care or test "not medically necessary."

If the procedure was miscoded because of a simple error, a simple letter from your doctor's office or a corrected treatment form can solve the problem and get you reimbursed.

Or maybe the billing code was put in intentionally, but was inaccurate. There are so many diagnostic codes that the one, which most accurately describes your condition, may not have been assigned the first time around.

Other times, a procedure code was inserted without the justifying diagnosis. A letter that explains the diagnosis can justify the procedure and get you a check.

Don't hesitate to call your doctor and ask for supporting documentation. He or she can explain why the procedure was medically necessary or help you justify why a specific treatment option was chosen.

Whatever the reason your claim was turned down, here are some sample letters you can use to communicate with your insurance company and medical care providers. Just fill in the specifics for your situation, and send it off via fax or mail. Don't forget to include documentation from your physician (referral forms, treatment forms, etc.) and don't forget to keep a copy of everything for yourself. If you already paid, enclose copies of receipts as well as cancelled checks, if you still have them.

Always verify the fax number or mailing address and always send your letter to a specific person. Letters may need to be sent to a national rather than local office, and you want the letter to get into the right hands right away. If you don't have a specific person, you won't know who to call to follow up.

INCORRECT PROCEDURE CODE

[DATE]

[PERSON NAME]
[INSURANCE COMPANY NAME]
[INSURANCE COMPANY ADDRESS OR FAX #]

RE: [YOUR NAME]
  [YOUR POLICY NUMBER AND SOCIAL SECURITY NUMBER]
  [NAME OF DEPENDENT IF CLAIM IS ABOUT DEPENDENT INSTEAD OF SELF]

DEAR [NAME]:
  I am writing about your denial of claim #____ on [DATE].
  Please note that there was an error in the procedure code listed by my physician's office. A letter/form identifying the correct code is attached.
  Please send me a check for the reimbursement as soon as possible. [OR: Please pay the fee to my physician's office as soon as possible.]
  Thank you.
Sincerely,

[YOUR NAME]
ENCL: [LIST ALL ENCLOSURES]

REFERRALS

[DATE]

[PERSON NAME]
[INSURANCE COMPANY NAME]
[INSURANCE COMPANY ADDRESS OR FAX #]

RE: [YOUR NAME]
   [YOUR POLICY NUMBER AND SOCIAL SECURITY NUMBER]
   [NAME OF DEPENDENT IF CLAIM IS ABOUT DEPENDENT INSTEAD OF SELF]

DEAR [NAME]:
   I am writing about your denial of claim #_____ on [DATE].
   Your letter [OR: name of person at insurance company] explained that my claim was turned down because you had no record of a written referral from my primary care physician.
   A copy of that referral is enclosed.
   Please send me a check for the reimbursement as soon as possible. [OR: Please pay the fee to Dr. _____ as soon as possible.]
   Thank you.
Sincerely,

[YOUR NAME]
ENCL: [LIST ALL ENCLOSURES]

DUPLICATE CHARGE-HOSPITAL

[DATE]

[PERSON NAME]
[HOSPITAL NAME]
[HOSPITAL ADDRESS OR FAX #]

RE: [YOUR NAME]
   [YOUR POLICY NUMBER AND SOCIAL SECURITY NUMBER]
   [NAME OF DEPENDENT IF CLAIM IS ABOUT DEPENDENT INSTEAD OF SELF]

DEAR [NAME]:
   I am writing about the enclosed invoice dated ____.
   The invoice includes several charges, which I have been billed for separately. [Detail all duplicate charges: surgeon, anesthesiologist, etc.]
   Copies of those paid invoices are enclosed.
   Please have these duplicate charges removed from my bill.
   Thank you.
Sincerely,

[YOUR NAME]
ENCL: [LIST ALL ENCLOSURES]

DUPLICATE CHARGE-DOCTOR/HOSPITAL

[DATE]

[PERSON NAME]
[DOCTOR'S OFFICE NAME]
[ADDRESS OR FAX #]

RE: [YOUR NAME]
    [YOUR POLICY NUMBER AND SOCIAL SECURITY NUMBER]
    [NAME OF DEPENDENT IF CLAIM IS ABOUT DEPENDENT
INSTEAD OF SELF]

DEAR [NAME]:
    I am writing about the enclosed invoice dated _____.
    Your fees were included on a lump sum bill from the hospital that
has already been paid.
    A copies of that paid invoice is enclosed.
    Please have the charge removed from my account.
    Thank you.
Sincerely,

[YOUR NAME]
ENCL: [LIST ALL ENCLOSURES]

DUPLICATE CHARGE-DOCTOR'S OFFICE

[DATE]

[PERSON NAME]
[DOCTOR'S OFFICE NAME]
[ADDRESS OR FAX #]

RE: [YOUR NAME]
    [YOUR POLICY NUMBER AND SOCIAL SECURITY NUMBER]
    [NAME OF DEPENDENT IF CLAIM IS ABOUT DEPENDENT INSTEAD OF SELF]

DEAR [NAME]:
    I am writing about the enclosed invoice dated _____.
    The invoice includes several charges, which I have been billed for separately by the lab. [Detail all duplicate charges: x-rays, blood tests, etc.]
    Copies of those paid invoices are enclosed.
    Please have those duplicate charges removed from my bill.
    Thank you.
Sincerely,

[YOUR NAME]
ENCL: [LIST ALL ENCLOSURES]

DUPLICATE CHARGE-LAB

[DATE]

[PERSON NAME]
[LAB NAME]
[LAB ADDRESS OR FAX #]

RE: [YOUR NAME]
    [YOUR POLICY NUMBER AND SOCIAL SECURITY NUMBER]
    [NAME OF DEPENDENT IF CLAIM IS ABOUT DEPENDENT
INSTEAD OF SELF]

DEAR [NAME]:
    I am writing about the enclosed invoice dated _____.
    The invoice has already been billed to my insurance company,
[NAME OF INSURANCE COMPANY & POLICY NUMBER].
    According to [NAME OF PERSON] at [NAME OF INSURANCE
COMPANY], the bill was paid on [OR: will be paid on] [DATE].
    Please have these duplicate charges removed from my bill.
    Thank you.
Sincerely,

[YOUR NAME]
ENCL: [LIST ALL ENCLOSURES]

ERRONEOUS HOSPITAL CHARGES

[DATE]

[PERSON NAME]
[HOSPITAL NAME]
[HOSPITAL ADDRESS OR FAX #]

RE: [YOUR NAME]
  [YOUR POLICY NUMBER AND SOCIAL SECURITY NUMBER]
  [NAME OF DEPENDENT IF CLAIM IS ABOUT DEPENDENT INSTEAD OF SELF]

DEAR [NAME]:
  I am writing about the enclosed invoice dated ____.
  The invoice includes several erroneous charges.
  [Detail all erroneous charges: a specialist who never reviewed your case, five daily doctor visits when the doctor showed up only twice, lab tests you didn't have, charges that belong to other patients, co-payments for twelve days when the policy limit is five, etc.]
  Please have these charges removed from my bill.
  Thank you.
Sincerely,

[YOUR NAME]
ENCL: [LIST ALL ENCLOSURES]

NOT COVERED

[DATE]

[PERSON NAME]
[INSURANCE COMPANY NAME]
[INSURANCE COMPANY ADDRESS OR FAX #]

RE: [YOUR NAME]
   [YOUR POLICY NUMBER AND SOCIAL SECURITY NUMBER]
   [NAME OF DEPENDENT IF CLAIM IS ABOUT DEPENDENT
INSTEAD OF SELF]

DEAR [NAME]:
   I am writing about your denial of claim #____ on [DATE].
   Your letter [OR: name of person at insurance company] explained that my claim was turned down because the service [OR: test or procedure] is not covered.
   But according to my policy [OR: summary of benefits], which I have attached, it is covered. [QUOTE THE POLICY ON COVERAGE. If you meet specific conditions like age, family history or previous test results, highlight them.]
   Please send me a check for the reimbursement as soon as possible. [OR: Please pay the fee to my physician's office/the hospital/the lab as soon as possible.]
   Thank you.
Sincerely,

[YOUR NAME]
ENCL: [LIST ALL ENCLOSURES]

NOT MEDICALLY NECESSARY

[DATE]

[PERSON NAME]
[INSURANCE COMPANY NAME]
[INSURANCE COMPANY ADDRESS OR FAX #]

RE: [YOUR NAME]
   [YOUR POLICY NUMBER AND SOCIAL SECURITY NUMBER]
   [NAME OF DEPENDENT IF CLAIM IS ABOUT DEPENDENT INSTEAD OF SELF]

DEAR [NAME]:
   I am writing about your denial of claim #____ on [DATE].
   Your letter [OR: name of person at insurance company] explained that my claim was turned down because the treatment/procedure was not medically necessary.
   A letter from my physician, Dr. _____, is enclosed, justifying the treatment/procedure.
   Please send me a check for the reimbursement as soon as possible. [OR: Please pay the fee to my physician's office as soon as possible.]
   Thank you.
   Sincerely,

[YOUR NAME]
ENCL: [LIST ALL ENCLOSURES]

EMERGENCY CARE

[DATE]

[PERSON NAME]
[INSURANCE COMPANY NAME]
[INSURANCE COMPANY ADDRESS OR FAX #]

RE: [YOUR NAME]
   [YOUR POLICY NUMBER AND SOCIAL SECURITY NUMBER]
   [NAME OF DEPENDENT IF CLAIM IS ABOUT DEPENDENT
INSTEAD OF SELF]

DEAR [NAME]:
   I am writing about your denial of claim #_____ on [DATE].
   Your letter [OR: name of person at insurance company] explained
that my situation was not an emergency and therefore not covered.
   The Health Insurance Portability and Accountability Act of 1996
mandates that individuals must have access to emergency care, without
prior authorization, in any situation that a "prudent lay person" would
regard as an emergency.
   [Include brief description of the medical situation.]
   Please send me a check for the reimbursement as soon as possible.
[OR: Please pay the fee to the hospital/clinic as soon as possible.]
   Thank you.
Sincerely,

[YOUR NAME]
ENCL: [LIST ALL ENCLOSURES]

PRE-EXISTING CONDITIONS

[DATE]

[PERSON NAME]
[INSURANCE COMPANY NAME]
[INSURANCE COMPANY ADDRESS OR FAX #]

RE: [YOUR NAME]
   [YOUR POLICY NUMBER AND SOCIAL SECURITY NUMBER]
   [NAME OF DEPENDENT IF CLAIM IS ABOUT DEPENDENT INSTEAD OF SELF]

DEAR [NAME]:
   I am writing about your denial of claim #_____ on [DATE].
   Your letter [OR: name of person at insurance company] explained that my condition was pre-existing and therefore not covered.
   I have had continuous healthcare coverage for over 12 months. [Enclose documentation.] According to the Health Insurance Portability and Accountability Act of 1996, insurance companies may not deny coverage for pre-existing conditions when an individual has had healthcare coverage for at least 12 continuous months.
   Please send me a check for the reimbursement as soon as possible. [OR: Please pay the fee to the doctor/hospital/clinic/lab as soon as possible.]
   Thank you.
Sincerely,

[YOUR NAME]
ENCL: [LIST ALL ENCLOSURES]

RECONSTRUCTIVE SURGERY

[DATE]

[PERSON NAME]
[INSURANCE COMPANY NAME]
[INSURANCE COMPANY ADDRESS OR FAX #]

RE: [YOUR NAME]
   [YOUR POLICY NUMBER AND SOCIAL SECURITY NUMBER]
   [NAME OF DEPENDENT IF CLAIM IS ABOUT DEPENDENT INSTEAD OF SELF]

DEAR [NAME]:
   I am writing about your denial of claim #____ on [DATE].
   Your letter [OR: name of person at insurance company] explained that my reconstruction after my mastectomy was "not medically necessary," and therefore not covered.
   The Women's Health and Cancer Rights Act of 1998 mandates that insurers pay the costs of reconstructive surgery after mastectomies.
   Please send me a check for the reimbursement as soon as possible. [OR: Please pay the fee to the doctor/hospital as soon as possible.]
   Thank you.
Sincerely,

[YOUR NAME]
ENCL: [LIST ALL ENCLOSURES]

CHILDBIRTH STAY

[DATE]

[PERSON NAME]
[INSURANCE COMPANY NAME]
[INSURANCE COMPANY ADDRESS OR FAX #]

RE: [YOUR NAME]
   [YOUR POLICY NUMBER AND SOCIAL SECURITY NUMBER]
   [NAME OF DEPENDENT IF CLAIM IS ABOUT DEPENDENT INSTEAD OF SELF]

DEAR [NAME]:
   I am writing about your denial of claim #_____ on [DATE].
   Your letter [OR: name of person at insurance company] denied full payment for my hospital stay when I gave birth to my baby.
   According to the Newborns' and Mothers' Protection Act, you must pay for a 48-hour stay after childbirth for a normal delivery [Or: 96 hours after a cesarean section].
   Please send me a check for the reimbursement as soon as possible. [OR: Please pay the fee to the hospital as soon as possible.]
   Thank you.
Sincerely,

[YOUR NAME]
ENCL: [LIST ALL ENCLOSURES]

HOSPITALIZATION

[DATE]

[PERSON NAME]
[INSURANCE COMPANY NAME]
[INSURANCE COMPANY ADDRESS OR FAX #]

RE: [YOUR NAME]
    [YOUR POLICY NUMBER AND SOCIAL SECURITY NUMBER]
    [NAME OF DEPENDENT IF CLAIM IS ABOUT DEPENDENT
INSTEAD OF SELF]

DEAR [NAME]:
    I am writing about your denial of claim #_____ on [DATE].
    Your letter [OR: name of person at insurance company] denied full
payment for my hospital stay when [add details].
    According to [federal or state law], I am entitled to [specify coverage].
    Please send me a check for the reimbursement as soon as possible.
[OR: Please pay the fee to the hospital as soon as possible.]
    Thank you.
Sincerely,

[YOUR NAME]
ENCL: [LIST ALL ENCLOSURES]

CHAPTER 26—WORKSHEET: FILL-IN-THE-BLANKS FORMS TO RECONCILE YOUR MEDICAL BILLS AND INSURANCE PAYMENTS

The reason for charting your payments and expenses is to see where you are being overcharged, double-billed or not credited for payments you already made. You can't know you deserve a refund if you haven't figured out you've been overcharged, so you need a simple way to track your medical costs.

We'll make it easy for you. Just look at the sample worksheets at the end of this chapter, then use the fill-in-the-blanks worksheets for your medical costs, co-payments and deductibles. The overcharges and refunds due will be laid out right in front of you in black and white.

Each time you get a bill, make a payment or receive a benefits statement from your insurance company, just jot the amounts in the worksheet and do the math. The errors will stare you in the face, often before you pay them. The earlier chapters in the book tell you how to identify the problems, get erroneous charges cancelled and have overpayments refunded to you; this worksheet will help you identify them when they happen for easy tracking. You'll have all the information you need to avoid overpaying for your medical care.

You can not only chart the numbers for current costs and start obtaining refunds now, you can easily go back several years. Just pull out your old bills, receipts and cancelled checks, enter the numbers in the worksheet, and add up your refunds.

It may take a little time, but it's worth it. Remember, the healthcare industry is a trillion-dollar business that makes close to $40 billion in errors every year. Get your part of it.

STEP 1:   You must know your policy. Read your summary of benefits. I if you don't already have it, also get your benefits booklet from your company Human Resources Administrator or your insurer to fully understand your coverage. If it's not clear, call customer service at your insurance company and ask questions until you understand your benefits. Your summary of benefits is a great place to start, but you'll need the comprehensive benefits booklet to make sure you get every dollar you are entitled to. For example, you may be entitled to a well-woman or dermatology exam every year without a referral. Or you may pay a lot less with a participating hospital. Your benefits booklet will explain this.

STEP 2:   Compare your policy with your medical bills and your benefits statement from your insurance company. If you do not get a statement, call the provider first; the office may not have submitted your bill to the insurance company. Or your insurance company may not have properly processed your bill. With the medical providers' invoice, you can easily reconcile the information whenever there is a discrepancy: you were charged full price when your policy guarantees reasonable and customary rates; you already met your annual deductible, but your insurer neglected to calculate that. Simply enter it on the worksheet, discover the error, and call the doctor, hospital, lab or insurance company to have it corrected.

STEP 3: Whenever you deal with anyone, write down the direct telephone number, extension, date, name [first and last] and title of that person. *This is very important.* If they promise certain results in a certain period of time [a copy of the bill in one week, a charge removed from your account in ten days], follow up to make sure it was done. Since you have the person's name and phone extension in your notes, you can easily call and refer back to what was said.

STEP 4: Follow up. Follow up. Follow up: on the phone and in writing—until the error is resolved. One call doesn't always do it, but persistence pays off in big dollars. Keep after them until either the charge is corrected on your account or you receive your refund.

STEP 5: Refer back to the earlier chapters whenever you need to. They tell you what type of errors to look out for. If the codes or the amounts charged on the bills from your providers do not match the figures on your insurance benefits statement, you have an error. You may be getting charged for a more expensive procedure because of a typo or denied coverage completely because a referral form is missing. Or the coverage may be turned down because you were billed for an unapproved procedure you didn't even have.

HOW TO USE THE WORKSHEET:

Since there's more than one way to look at things, we're giving you more than one option. The worksheet is designed several different ways; use whichever layout works best for you.

Every time you have a healthcare expense, enter the information on the chart. Simple arithmetic will tell you where you stand. It's easy to track your medical costs and determine who owes you how much money.

Since HMOs are such simple plans, with minor co-payments for medical services, charts aren't necessary. The previous chapters, which detail how to avoid overpayments and get refunds for double-billing, decipher unitemized bills, demand required coverage, etc., tell you all you need to keep your medical costs down to what you really owe.

Since PPO and POS plans are a bit more complex, the following worksheet will help you track your costs, overpayments and refunds due. Each entry in the sample worksheet is followed by an explanation.

The worksheet also tallies a running year-to-date total at the bottom of the page, so you'll see exactly when you hit your annual deductible and annual out-of-pocket limits. Deductibles are a set dollar amount like $500 per person or $1500 per family. Annual out-of-pocket limits are usually equal to the total of your co-payments, not including pharmacy costs. Check with your insurer on how it's calculated for on your specific plan.

You can easily customize the worksheet to your particular situation. Add or delete columns if necessary for your particular situation. If you don't have a cafeteria plan, for example, you can just take it out.

If you do have a cafeteria plan, you can be reimbursed for all medical costs your insurer has not paid for, up to the maximum of your annual contributions. Cafeteria plans reimburse for out-of-pocket fees, whether or not you paid full price or reasonable customary fees. Your reimbursement will be the amount you paid, minus the amount you were reimbursed by your insurer. Cafeteria plans also reimburse for medical expenses, like eyeglasses, dental care and therapy, that may not be covered by your health insurance policy.

SAMPLE WORKSHEET #1
75

EXAMPLE #	DESCRIPTION	AMOUNT CHARGED	R & C	DEDUCT	CO-PAY	YOU PAID PROVIDER	PROVIDER OWES YOU	YOU OWE PROVIDER	CAFETERIA
1.	Office Visit	80	55	55	–	80	25	–	55

You paid $80 for an office visit, but the reasonable and customary cost was only $55. Since it's the beginning of the year and you haven't yet applied anything to your $500 annual deductible, the entire $55 goes to your deductible. **(The doctor owes you the $25 you overpaid.)**

EXAMPLE #	DESCRIPTION	AMOUNT CHARGED	R & C	DEDUCT	CO-PAY	YOU PAID PROVIDER	PROVIDER OWES YOU	YOU OWE PROVIDER	CAFETERIA
2.	Office Visit	80	55	55	–	80	25	–	55

This is the same as example #1. An additional $55 goes to your annual deductible. Your cafeteria plan will reimburse you for your $55 out-of-pocket cost. **(The doctor owes you the $25 you overpaid.)**

EXAMPLE #	DESCRIPTION	AMOUNT CHARGED	R & C	DEDUCT	CO-PAY	YOU PAID PROVIDER	PROVIDER OWES YOU	YOU OWE PROVIDER	CAFETERIA
3.	Office Visit	80	55	55	–	55	–	–	55

By this visit, you know you were overcharged at the doctor's office the first two times, so you paid only the reasonable and customary fee of $55. With those three visits, you'd paid $165 [$55 x 3] toward your annual deductible, meaning you will only get reimbursements after you pay another $335. Your cafeteria plan will reimburse you for your $165 out-of-pocket cost.

EXAMPLE #	DESCRIPTION	AMOUNT CHARGED	R & C	DEDUCT	CO-PAY	YOU PAID PROVIDER	PROVIDER OWES YOU	YOU OWE PROVIDER	CAFETERIA
4.	TEST	575	385	335	10	–	–	345	345

You were charged $575 for a diagnostic test, but the reasonable and customary fee was only $385. $335 is applied toward the remainder of your $500 deductible. You will pay only 20% of the remainder of the reasonable and customary fee: $50 x 20% = $10, plus the $335 of the $345, to the provider. Your cafeteria plan will reimburse you for your $345 out-of-pocket cost.

5. Office Visit	80	55	–	11	11	–	11

You only have to pay the $11 co-payment [20% of $55], since you fulfilled your annual deductible. As you paid the $11 co-payment at the office, you don't owe anything more. Your cafeteria plan will reimburse you for your $11 out-of-pocket cost.

6. Hospital Room	2400	1600	–	320	1000	680	–	320

Examples 6 through 9 all deal with a hospitalization. Often, before a hospitalization, the doctor or hospital asks for some payment up front. The amount often has little to do with what the final costs will be, so they may owe you a lot of money or vice versa. In this example, you paid $1000, but the reasonable and customary fee for this $2400 procedure is only $1600. Your share is 20% of the $1600 or $320. You paid $320, so the hospital owes you $680. Your cafeteria plan will reimburse you for your $320 out-of-pocket cost.

7. Surgery	8000	7000	*1159	3500	2341	–	1159

Your reasonable and customary fee for your surgery is $7000. Normally, you would pay your co-payment of 20% [$1400]. In this case, you already paid $341 toward your annual out-of-pocket maximum of $1500. Therefore, your co-payment in this case would only be $1159 [$1500 - $341 = $1159]. Now your insurance company will pay the rest of your claims for the year at 100%. You paid $3,500 so the hospital owes you $2341. Your cafeteria plan will reimburse you for your $1159 out-of-pocket cost.

(Continued On Next Page)

8. Operating Room	4000	3200	—	—	—	—	—
9. Hospital Room	2400	1600	—	—	—	—	—

Since you haven't advanced the hospital any money and you met your annual out-of-pocket maximum, your cost is nothing.

This is the same as example #8.

ANNUAL TOTALS TO DATE	17,695	14,005	500	1,500	4726	3071	345	2000

* You have reached your annual out-of-pocket maximum, $1500 with this plan, so you don't have to pay anymore.

Note: *In most cases you will continually be logging in office visit after office visit. If you have a family plan, 20-50 office visits per year are commonplace. If you have a child or adult getting weekly treatments or monitoring for asthma, allergy or diabetes, this could easy push the number of visits to 80 or 100 a year.*

FILL-IN-THE-BLANKS WORKSHEET #1A

EXAMPLE #	DESCRIPTION	AMOUNT CHARGED	R & C	DEDUCT	CO-PAY	YOU PAID PROVIDER	PROVIDER OWES YOU	YOU OWE PROVIDER	CAFETERIA
1.									
2.									
3.									
4.									
5.									
6.									
7.									
8.									

SAMPLE WORKSHEET #1B

This worksheet contains the same information as 1A but displayed vertically instead of horizontally. Use whichever layout works best for you.

										TOTAL
YOUR PROVIDER CHARGES YOU	80	80	80	575	80	2400	8000	4000	2400	**17695**
REASONABLE & CUSTOMARY (+)	55	55	55	385	55	1600	7000	3200	1600	**14005**
TOWARD YOUR DEDUCTIBLE (+)	55	55	55	335	–	–	–	–	–	**500**
YOUR CO-PAY IS 20% [R & C – deductible x 20%] (+)	–	–	–	10	11	320	1159	–	–	**1500**
YOU PAID YOUR PROVIDER (–)	80	80	55	–	11	1000	3500	–	–	**4726**
YOU RECEIVED FROM INSURER (+)										
TOTAL	-25	-25	--	345	--	-680	-2341	--	--	
PROVIDER OWES YOU	25	25	--	–	–	680	2341	–	–	**3071**
YOU OWE YOUR PROVIDER	--	--	–	345	--	–	–	–	–	**345**
CAFETERIA	55	55	55	345	11	320	1159	–	–	**2000**

FILL-IN-THE-BLANKS WORKSHEET #1B

This worksheet contains the same information as 1A but displayed vertically instead of horizontally. Use whichever layout works best for you.

YOUR PROVIDER CHARGES YOU						
REASONABLE & CUSTOMARY						
TOWARD YOUR DEDUCTIBLE						
YOUR CO-PAY IS 20% [R & C - deductible x 20%]						
YOU PAID YOUR PROVIDER						
YOU RECEIVED FROM INSURER						

TOTAL						

PROVIDER OWES YOU						
YOU OWE YOUR PROVIDER						
CAFETERIA						

SAMPLE WORKSHEET #2

This worksheet shows the same medical event [a $40 office visit] in a variety of different situations. In some scenarios you already paid the provider, in others you didn't. Just follow the columns and you will quickly see what you owe or how much you are owed.

YOUR PROVIDER CHARGES YOU	40	40	40	40	40	40
REASONABLE & CUSTOMARY +	30.50	30.50	30.50	30.50	30.50	30.50
TOWARD YOUR DEDUCTIBLE +	30.50	30.50	25	25	--	--
YOUR CO-PAY IS 20% + [R & C - deductible x 20%]	--	--	1.10	1.10	6.10	6.10
YOU PAID YOUR PROVIDER -	--	40	--	40	--	40
YOU RECEIVED FROM INSURER +	--	--	--	--	--	--
TOTAL	+30.50	-9.50	+26.10	-13.90	+6.10	-33.90

FILL-IN-THE-BLANKS WORKSHEET #2

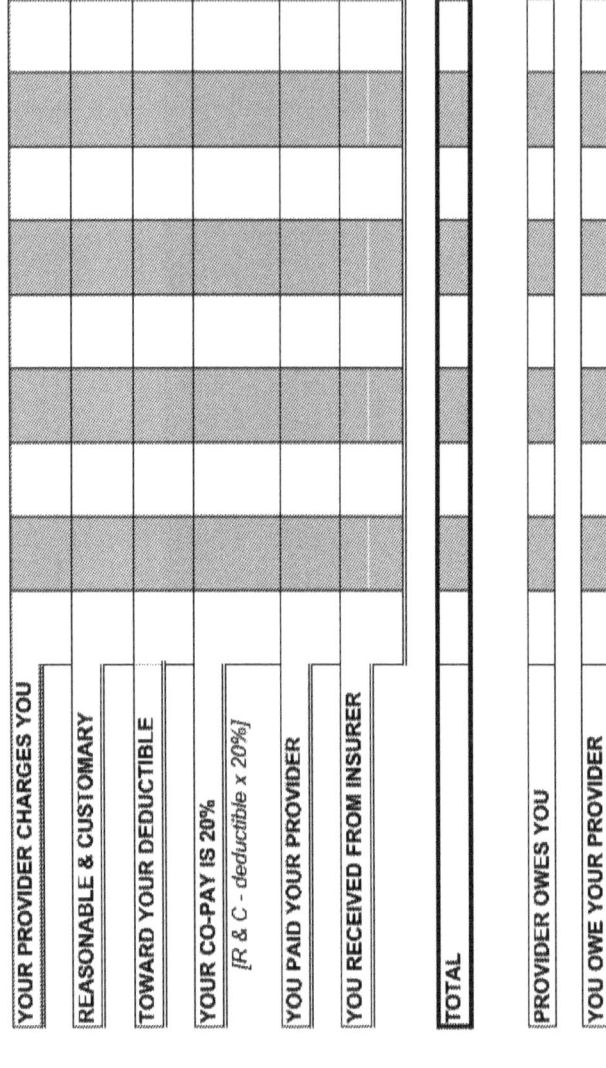

YOUR PROVIDER CHARGES YOU							
REASONABLE & CUSTOMARY							
TOWARD YOUR DEDUCTIBLE							
YOUR CO-PAY IS 20% [R & C - deductible x 20%]							
YOU PAID YOUR PROVIDER							
YOU RECEIVED FROM INSURER							

TOTAL	

PROVIDER OWES YOU	
YOU OWE YOUR PROVIDER	

CHAPTER 27—COMPARATIVE WORKSHEETS: WHAT PLAN IS BEST FOR YOU?

Although there is no absolute way to compare all policies because there are so many variables, this worksheet shows you how to approach a policy comparison for any type of policy.

Do you want to compare an HMO, a PPO, a POS, a catastrophic plan, even different levels of deductibles? Just estimate your annual medical care, based on past experience and your current health, put it on the worksheet, along with the costs of the various premiums, and you'll have an easy time making your choice. HMO plans are switching back to PPO/POS plans at any astonishing rate of almost 3% per year, so they're worth taking another look at.

Look at how much money you can save, but don't let your comparison be limited to numbers. Money is important, but the most important thing is that you are comfortable with the medical care providers on your plan. Look also at other intangibles: can you see a specialist without a referral; do you prefer an HMO to a PPO so you won't have to make a big payment for each doctor visit; do you want to see any doctor you chose, no matter what it costs?

Insurance costs have risen so dramatically in the last five years, to thousands of dollars per year, per person, just for premiums—before you've received any medical care—that catastrophic or high deductible policies are becoming the most cost effective policies on the market for many people.

These policies have higher deductibles and higher co-payments, offset by much lower monthly premiums. What you save in premiums is more than most people spend on doctor visits in a year, so you can really come out ahead. Unless you have a chronic condition, and you know you'll need a lot of medical care during the year, high deductible policies can be the best deal.

A PPO may give you a broader choice of doctors than an HMO. If that's more important to you than cost, how much you save is secondary. But if money and cost control outweighs choice for you, than an HMO might be a better choice. Once you fill in the worksheet, it will be easier to identify the plan that is best for you.

The sample worksheet will show you how to compare. We assumed 20, then 30 doctor visits per year for your family. That may be more times that you'd go in a year, but if that's the case, your costs will actually be a lot less. When filling in the worksheet, estimate five or twenty or fifty visits, whatever seems realistic for you. If you anticipate a hospitalization, put that in, too.

With a traditional policy, your monthly family cost based on 20 annual visits to the doctor with prescriptions can be as high as $7620 or $381 per visit. With a catastrophic policy, you deductible may be $3,000 per person or $7,000 per family, instead of $300 or $900 per person, but your monthly premiums will decrease drastically.

If you had a policy that cost a little more than half the monthly premium but you paid for the 20 visits yourself, as you would with a catastrophic policy, the cost per visit would be $255 per visit or a substantial savings of $2580 a year. The attached comparative worksheet shows you how.

You can use the following comparative spreadsheet to not only see what the "true" cost of your insurance is, but to see which kind of policy offers the best deal for you.

Comparative Worksheet

	PLAN 1		PLAN2	
	900 Deductible		3000 Deductible	
Monthly Premium	$ 550		$ 300	
Annual Cost	$ 6,600		$ 3,600	
Assume 20 Visits @ 175/visit				
12 X $75 (Deductible met)	$ 900	20 visits @ $75	$ 1,500	
8 X $15 co-pay	$ 120			
Total Annual Cost	$ 7,620		$ 5,100	
Cost per visit	$ 381		$ 255	
Annual Premium Cost	$ 6,600		$ 3,600	
Assume 30 Visits @ 75/visit		30 visits @ $75	$ 2,250	
12 visits @ $75	$ 900			
18 visits @ $15	$ 270			
Total Annual Cost	$ 7,770		$ 5,850	
Cost per visit	$ 259		$ 195	
Annual Premium Cost	$ 6,600		$ 3,600	
Assume 20 Visits @ 50/visit		20 visits @ $50	$ 1,000	
18 visits @ $50	$ 900			
2 visits @ $10	$ 20			
Total Annual Cost	$ 7,520		$ 4,600	
Cost per visit	$ 376		$ 230	

Comparative Worksheet

PLAN 1

_____ Deductible

Monthly Premium $ _____

Annual Cost $ _____

Assume 20 Visits @ 175/visit [*or another amount

12 X $75 (Deductible met) $ _____

8 X $_____ co-pay $ _____

Total Annual Cost $ _____

Cost per visit $ _____

PLAN2

_____ Deductible

$ _____

$ _____

20 visits @ $75 $ _____

$ _____

$ _____

* You can use a different amount, depending on the average cost per visit to a doctor in your area. Use last year's fees as a guideline, or call up your own medical care providers and ask what the reasonable and customary fees are. Remember that specialists cost more than primary care physicians, and lab tests and diagnostic tests, if required, may cost extra.